Congress,
the Executive Branch,
and
National Security

THE NEW TUG-OF-WAR

Jeremy D. Rosner

A CARNEGIE ENDOWMENT BOOK

© Copyright 1995
Carnegie Endowment for International Peace
2400 N Street, N.W.
Washington, D.C. 20037
Tel. (202) 862-7900
Fax (202) 862-2610

The New Tug-Of-War: Congress, the Executive Branch, and National Security may be ordered from the Brookings Institution, Department 029, Washington, DC 20041-0029, USA, Tel. 1/800-275-1447.

Design by Barbara Shear.
Printed by Automated Graphic Systems.

Library of Congress Cataloging-in-Publication Data

Rosner, Jeremy D., 1958-
p. cm.
ISBN: 0-87003-062-0 (pbk.)
1. National security—United States.
2. United States—Military policy.
3. United States. Congress.
4. Executive power—United States. I. Title
UA23.R763 1995   95-17583
                                                   CIP

Contents

Introduction

Congress creates a program to aid Russian denuclearization; it cuts off funding for the U.S. military mission in Somalia; it forces the president to pursue an alternative plan for responding to Mexico's peso crisis. As this book goes to press, Congress is acting on legislation that would cut back America's foreign aid program, shut down three agencies that administer aspects of U.S. foreign policy, and provide policy guidance or restrictions regarding Russia, China, Taiwan, North Korea, and a host of other countries. Much as the press and public at any point in time may speak of "the administration's foreign policy," these and many other recent events remind us that American national security policy, like a divining rod, is driven by two branches, not just one.[1]

This was the founders' design. The Constitution makes the president commander-in-chief and gives him the dominant voice in diplomacy; it empowers Congress to fund foreign programs, raise armies, approve treaties, regulate trade, confirm nominees, and declare war.[2] The Constitution created an "invitation to struggle for the privilege of directing American foreign policy," in the words of E. S. Corwin.[3] The character of this struggle makes a difference. Clear debate over critical choices can improve pro-

---

[1] There is an energetic scholarly debate about the nature, extent, and value of Congress's influence on U.S. national security policy. Some of the major recent works are: Barry M. Blechman, *The Politics of National Security* (Oxford University Press, 1990); L. Gordon Crovitz and Jeremy A. Rabkin, eds., *The Fettered Presidency: Legal Constraints on the Executive Branch* (American Enterprise Institute, 1990); Barbara Hinckley, *Less than Meets the Eye* (University of Chicago Press, 1994); Thomas M. Franck and Edward Weisband, *Foreign Policy by Congress* (Oxford University Press, 1979); James M. Lindsay, *Congress and the Politics of U.S. Foreign Policy* (The Johns Hopkins University Press, 1994); Thomas E. Mann, ed., *A Question of Balance: The President, the Congress and Foreign Policy* (The Brookings Institution, 1990). The literature is well summarized in: James M. Lindsay and Randall B. Ripley, "Foreign and Defense Policy in Congress: A Research Agenda for the 1990s," *Legislative Studies Quarterly*, vol. XVII, No. 3 (August 1992), pp. 417-49.

[2] Members of both branches influence national security decisions in indirect ways as well—for example, by appearing on news programs. See: James M. Lindsay, "Congress, Foreign Policy, and the New Institutionalism," International Studies Quarterly, Vol. 38 (June 1994), pp. 281-304.

[3] Edward S. Corwin, *The President: Office and Powers*, 1787-1957 (New York University Press, 1957), p. 171.

grams and strengthen public understanding. Extreme discord can weaken U.S. credibility abroad.

Countless analyses have examined how the end of the Cold War is transforming the country's security environment. Yet relatively little has been written about how the end of the Cold War is changing the tug-of-war between the executive branch and Congress and how those changes affect the country's responses to a new world.

To the extent Congress figures in analyses of U.S. national security policy (defined here as defense, intelligence, trade, and foreign policy), the focus is on the dramatic turnover in partisan control of Capitol Hill after the 1994 elections. The Republican capture of both the House and the Senate has brought an entirely new cast of committee chairmen, many of whom are the ideological opposites of their Democratic predecessors. Policy differences abound across the aisle. There is now more enthusiasm for defense spending, less for foreign aid. As the 1996 elections draw near, divided government gives Congress's Republican majority partisan reasons for criticizing the national security record of the Democratic president—just as congressional Democrats long criticized Republican presidents. And as the Republican Congress considers new cuts in international programs and new restrictions on the administration's foreign policies, the President and his top advisers have accused the GOP majority of advancing "the most isolationist proposals . . . in the last 50 years."[4]

But the partisan drama is only part of the story. This study contends that there are larger forces at work in the national security relationship between the two branches:

- Many of the diverse changes we are witnessing in the relationship between Congress and the executive on national security result from the end of the Cold War itself, not simply from partisan shifts. The dissolution of the Soviet Union removed the overarching strategic threat that the executive branch and members of Congress used to justify much of America's national security programs. The end of the Cold War also has contributed to other changes in the two branches' national security relationship, including heightened con-

---

[4] Statement by the President, May 23, 1995.

cern over domestic economics, budget pressures from high deficits, and an influx of new members of Congress.

- Generally, these changes will render Congress more assertive relative to the executive branch than during the late years of the Cold War. There is, of course, no accepted yardstick for measuring the strength of each branch, and the executive branch will continue to have the dominant voice in U.S. foreign relations. Yet in a less threatening world, with domestic concerns dominant, budget pressures high, and a flock of new members who came to Congress after the Cold War ended, Congress is more willing to challenge the executive branch's national security leadership. Congress's unwillingness to support President Clinton's proposed package of loan guarantees for Mexico in 1995—even when the White House asserted "vital interests" were at stake—may mark a watershed in relations between the branches on national security. Although changes in partisan control of the two branches do affect their relative power and shift the focus of contention to different issues, the tendency toward a stronger post-Cold War Congress is likely to hold true regardless of which party controls which branch.

- Although Congress is more assertive on national security since the end of the Cold War, that assertiveness is uneven and varies from issue to issue *in consistent ways.* In particular, Congress is notably less assertive when national security stakes in a particular issue appear to be high. The executive branch has an especially free hand when its policies have Cold War overtones, or produce domestic economic benefits, or when the White House has reached out to both parties in Congress. Recent examples include aid to former Soviet states and the North Korean nuclear agreement. When the national security stakes on an issue appear to be low, however, as on peacekeeping or development aid, Congress increasingly flexes its muscles. This divided pattern was clear *before* the Republicans took control of the Congress, and it is likely to continue.

- These changes in the executive-congressional relationship echo historical patterns. Throughout this century, the end of each major war changed the national security relationship between Congress and the executive. Whether Congress assumed a stronger or weaker role in national security depended on such factors as: perceptions of the war that had just ended; the new security threats that followed; the state of the economy after the war; and the extent to which the executive acted with bipartisanship toward Congress. Although the Cold War was different from the century's other major wars, these same factors still apply. Generally, these factors point to a slight increase in congressional assertiveness, while they also help single out the particular issues on which it is increasing most.

Soon after the 1994 elections swept Republicans into power in the Senate and House of Representatives, a prominent columnist argued that with the end of the Cold War, the time had come to boost the power of the presidency in national security policy: "A Republican Congress should return the foreign policy prerogatives that Democratic Congresses have taken from the White House."[5] The argument—echoing sentiments expressed by some in the early 1980s when the Republicans recaptured the White House and the Senate—assumes that the balance between the two branches on national security is primarily a matter of political choice and partisan calculation.[6] But this argument puts the cart before the horse. Presidential power in foreign affairs is a function of national danger. Relative peace on earth will tend to mean relatively less peace down the length of Pennsylvania Avenue.

Less than five years after the breakup of the Soviet Union, it is difficult to separate partisan changes from post-Cold War changes. With two parties, there are eight possible combinations of control of the Senate, House, and Oval Office. We have only seen three

---

[5] Charles Krauthammer, "Power to the President," *The Washington Post* (January 6, 1995), p. A21.

[6] For example, Senate Armed Services Committee chair John Tower wrote in 1981: "The 1970s were marked by a rash of Congressional initiated foreign policy legislation that limited the President's range of options.... [W]e must restore the traditional balance between Congress and the President.... To do so, much of the legislation of the past decade should be repealed or amended." "Congress versus the President: The Formulation and Implementation of American Foreign Policy," *Foreign Affairs* (Winter 1981/1982), pp. 234, 242.

combinations since the Berlin Wall fell: a Republican White House with a Democratic House and Senate; Democratic control of all three; and, since January 1995, a Democratic president with a Republican Congress. It may be too early to draw definite conclusions about what changes the end of the Cold War has brought to executive–congressional relations, apart from the changes caused by shifts in partisan control. It is still useful, however, to examine how Congress and the executive branch have fared on various national security issues in recent years and why.

This book opens with an overview of the current status and history of executive-congressional relations on national security policy. It then examines two recent case studies. The first is the Clinton administration's 1993 effort to provide an expanded package of assistance to Russia and the other new independent states (NIS) of the former Soviet Union. The second case is the administration's effort during 1993-94 to develop a new policy regarding multilateral peacekeeping and then to obtain the funds to support it. Both cases involved national security challenges that are hallmarks of the post-Cold War era and that have remained contentious as the 103rd Congress has given way to the 104th: support for reform in former communist states and multilateral peace operations. Yet the two cases turned out very differently. The Russia/NIS case suggests a powerful executive branch and a fully cooperative Congress; the peacekeeping case suggests a frustrated executive branch and a newly assertive Congress. A final chapter tries to explain this difference and to offer some prescriptions for the executive and Congress in the years ahead.

In these two cases, I do not attempt to evaluate whether the policies proposed by the executive branch or funded by Congress were wise or successful. To a large extent, the jury is still out. Instead, my aim is to lay out a broader thesis about how the relationship between the two branches is changing. Testing that thesis will require examination of more case studies and additional Congresses; the two cases here are offered as useful evidence, not conclusive proof.

The case analyses presented are based, in part, on over thirty interviews with people in the two branches who played key roles: members of Congress, congressional staff, and executive-branch officials. Virtually all of the executive officials were at the level of

Deputy Assistant Secretary or above. Almost all of the congressional staff were key aides for the leadership or relevant committees. The congressional members and staff included both Democrats and Republicans. To foster candor, I committed to withhold the names of the interview subjects.

Two definitions are necessary to clarify the comparisons this study makes between different periods of executive-congressional relations. First, it marks January 1992 as the beginning of the post-Cold War period. Clearly the Cold War began to thaw years earlier. Many bills before 1992 were post-Cold War in nature—for example the 1989 assistance package to Central Europe. Yet it was not until December 1991, with the last lowering of the Soviet flag over the Kremlin, that the Cold War reached its finale. Second, the study compares recent executive-congressional relations, not to the entire Cold War period, but only to the post-Vietnam portion of the Cold War, beginning with Gerald Ford's installation as president in August 1974 and running up until the beginning of 1989. These definitions leave a gap from the beginning of 1989 through the end of 1991, which is here viewed as a transitional period.

One caveat is in order. I cannot claim to approach this study as a wholly disinterested analyst. During the period examined in both the cases, I served as Counselor and Senior Director for Legislative Affairs on the staff of the National Security Council. In that capacity, I worked on both the 1993 assistance bill for Russia and the other NIS as well as the administration's efforts on peacekeeping. Some may conclude, as a result, that the case studies in this book are biased—that they attempt to exonerate views I held during the process or to grind some axe against bureaucratic rivals. This is not my intent. Rather, I chose these cases in part because my experience gave me some familiarity with them as well as a strong desire to understand better what was really happening while my colleagues and I muddled through the fog of congressional relations. If anything, these cases highlight missteps for which I bear substantial responsibility.

It is a confusing time in Congress and the executive branch. The end of the Cold War has deprived our elected officials of a single, overarching rationale for American internationalism. An uneven economy has increased pressures against foreign spending. The 1994 elections have turned the political landscape upside down. Even before these elections, votes on national security had often come to be characterized by odd and shifting coalitions. In such a political environment, there is a danger that our foreign policies and commitments will be unstable and that we will shrink from the leadership that is our responsibility as the world's greatest power. This is a clear concern of allies and friends abroad. If the United States is to be a respected partner and effective leader in the post-Cold War world, its executive and legislative branches must find new ways to mobilize public support around the nation's international programs and strategies. It is my hope that this study can assist in that process.

1 Executive-Congressional Relations on National Security After the Cold War

What are we to make of the jumble of recent legislative battles on national security—from human rights in China to the war in Bosnia, from NAFTA to the B-2 bomber? Are these and other fights simply products of partisan politics, or has the end of the Cold War itself changed the relationship between Congress and the executive branch in other, systematic ways?

To answer, we need to define more clearly three sets of transformations that have been occurring in executive-congressional relations since the end of the Cold War: 1) changes in the terms of debate; 2) changes in the balance of power between the branches; and 3) institutional and partisan changes within the two branches themselves.

Changes in the Focus and Terms of Debate

The most immediate consequence of the end of the Cold War for executive-congressional relations is also the most obvious one: As the Soviet threat disappeared from the globe, it also disappeared from the national security dialogue between the two branches. For example, throughout the post-Vietnam period of the Cold War (1974 to 1989), over 13 percent of "contested" national security votes involved opposition to communist governments or movements in the developing world.[1] Since 1992, there have been no

---

[1] "Contested" votes—which are a major focus of this study—denote those roll call votes on the floor of the House or Senate on which the executive branch declares a position, as recorded by *Congressional Quarterly* (*CQ*). *CQ*'s records on this question are not perfect. The journal determines whether or not an administration had a position on a vote primarily by referring to documents issued by the

footnote continued on page 10

contested votes on such issues. Similarly, as the end of the Soviet Union enabled an expansion in the number of peacekeeping missions worldwide, peacekeeping became an increasing focus of executive-legislative arguments, jumping from 2 percent of contested national security votes in 1974-89 to 12 percent in 1992-94 (21 percent, if one includes votes on Bosnia and Haiti).

In many ways, the end of the Cold War has changed the subjects of the national security debate less than the terms of debate. For example, from 1974 to 1989, votes on specific weapons systems accounted for 19 percent of contested national security votes; from 1992 through 1994, that figure was virtually the same, 20 percent. But now, debates over weapons systems such as missile defenses are argued not in terms of the Soviet deterrence, but in the context of regional conflicts and threats from rogue states. Similarly, U.S. intervention in the developing world remains a flash point, but now such missions are aimed at fostering regional stability (e.g., the Gulf War) or delivering humanitarian relief (e.g., Somalia) rather than stemming communist expansion (e.g., Nicaragua).

During the Cold War, issues between the two branches tended to revolve around the Soviet threat like spokes around the hub of

---

Office of Managementand Budget called "Statements of Administration Position." There are numerous cases, however, in which an administration did not issue such a document but nonetheless clearly took a public stand on a congressional vote—such as through press statements or by sending a letter from the president or other administration officials to members of Congress. This study relies on *CQ* records, however imperfect, because any effort to reconstruct administration positions over the past two decades would be subject to author bias. This focus on contested floor votes has many limitations: it ignores committee votes and omits issues that never reach the House or Senate floor, such as the SALT II treaty; it does not capture the negotiations between the branches that often shape what kinds of measures are brought to a vote; it ignores the other important ways in which Congress influences national security policy—for example, by framing issues in the media. On the limits of roll call vote analysis and the need for further research, see: James M. Lindsay and Wayne P. Steger, "The 'Two Presidencies' in Future Research: Moving Beyond Roll-Call Analysis," *Congress and the Presidency*, Vol. 20, No. 2 (Autumn 1993), pp. 103-17. Even among the set of contested votes identified by *CQ*, there is a question of which ones involve national security issues. This question is addressed in the Appendix. Finally, the term "contested" is not strictly accurate: Administrations sometimes declare their positions on uncontroversial resolutions—as in the case of the 1990 resolution condemning Iraq's invasion of Kuwait. In the vast majority of cases, however, administrations declare their positions on bills in order to increase congressional support.

a wheel. Since the end of the Cold War, the two branches have tended to address security issues as connected but separate, more like a pile of pick-up sticks.

Many writers and policymakers have tried to reassemble the sticks back around some central hub—to define a central idea for post-Cold War security policy, much as containment became the core idea during the Cold War. There have been several competitors in this "Kennan sweepstakes." President Bush invoked a "New World Order." President Clinton and his National Security Adviser, Anthony Lake, have argued that America's new central goal is the "enlargement" of the community of market democracies.[2]

As the debate over post-Cold War goals takes shape, old political alliances on national security are fracturing and odd new coalitions are emerging. In the effort to expand assistance to Russia and the other NIS, for example, there was opposition from both conservative Republicans, who were generally skeptical of foreign aid, and liberal Democrats, who preferred to spend the money on social programs at home. Fiscal conservatives and social liberals have joined forces in recent efforts to cut defense spending. Resolutions to lift the arms embargo on Bosnia have drawn support from human rights doves, anti-aggression hawks, and those who want to keep the United States out of the conflict altogether. Recent trade agreements and the 1995 package of Mexican loan guarantees fostered an opposition coalition that combined labor supporters, environmentalists, consumer advocates, populist independents, and conservative America First-ers, a coalition that made unlikeliest bedfellows of Ralph Nader, Ross Perot, and Pat Buchanan.

Many of the most dramatic changes in the terms of the national security debate involve economics. The United States, along with many other nations, has turned more attention to domestic economic and social concerns, which has led to a greater focus on

---

[2] Address by President Clinton to the 48th Session of the United Nations General Assembly, September 27, 1993; "From Containment to Enlargement," Remarks of Anthony Lake at the Johns Hopkins University School of Advanced International Studies, September 21, 1993.

the domestic economic consequences of its foreign policies.[3] For example, Sen. Mitch McConnell (R-KY), the new chair of the Senate Appropriations subcommittee on Foreign Operations, announced that one of three central principles for the 1995 foreign aid bill would be: "foreign aid must promote American economic interests"; he listed this objective ahead of the more traditional goal of "preserv[ing] political and regional stability."[4]

The new emphasis on economic concerns has affected issues on which domestic and foreign goals arguably collide. The rising weight of economic concerns was a significant factor in 1994, for example, when the Congress supported the Clinton administration's efforts to unlink China's trade status from its human rights performance. Similarly, beginning in 1991, Congress began to consider seriously a program to preserve U.S. defense jobs by subsidizing commercial arms sales to NATO members and other U.S. allies. Although the measure has yet to be enacted, it has drawn substantial support from many members who in the past expressed concern over arms proliferation and defense spending levels. The economic concerns of constituents, it would seem, are now relatively more important when members cast national security votes.

As a result, the relationship between the executive branch and Congress has changed on trade and international economics. While there has not been a surge in the number of key votes on trade, the politics of those votes has changed. The Democratic Party's movement away from free trade in recent decades was checked by the election of a Democratic president who campaigned for NAFTA and the new GATT agreement—a reflection, in part, of the rising importance of exports in the U.S. economy, as well as the declining power of organized labor. President Clinton's embrace of free trade fostered a bipartisan coalition in Congress that helped give his administration the most substantial two-year record of trade legislation in decades.[5] At the same time,

---

[3] See I. M. Destler, "Foreign Policy Making with the Economy at Center Stage," and Norman Ornstein, "Congress in the Post-Cold War World," both in Daniel Yankelovich and I. M. Destler, eds., *Beyond the Beltway: Engaging the Public in U.S. Foreign Policy* (The American Assembly/Norton, 1994).

[4] Press conference, December 12, 1994.

[5] The Clinton administration won five of five contested trade votes in the 103rd Congress. The Carter administration won five of five contested trade votes

global economic initiatives, which tend to create both economic winners and losers, have fueled a populist backlash and energized the new liberal-populist-reactionary coalition noted above.

Heightened concern over the deficit also has reshaped the national security debate in fundamental ways. Polls suggest that Americans view the deficit as the most important economic issue facing the country.[6] This concern has affected the politics of all federal activities, as suggested by the initial budget resolutions for FY1996 in the House and Senate, which aim to achieve a balanced budget by 2002. But, with the Cold War over, deficit reduction pressures have fallen disproportionately on national security programs. Budgets for defense and international affairs have fallen from 64 percent of discretionary spending (that is, spending apart from entitlements and interest on the debt) in FY1989 to 52 percent in FY1995. Most of the change stems from reductions in the defense outlays over this period from $304 billion to $272 billion (in nominal dollars).[7] Yet reductions in foreign aid under recent and proposed budgets also have been substantial. Sen. McConnell argued that, under the Senate's budget resolution for FY1996, "At the end of seven years, the United States would have as visible and viable an international role as Ghana."[8]

---

in the 96th Congress (1979-80), but two of Carter's five dealt only with specific sectors (wheat and sugar), whereas all five of the votes in the 103rd Congress were on multi-sector agreements (NAFTA and GATT). The Reagan administration compiled a 100 percent success rate on trade in the 97th Congress (1981-82), but there were only two contested votes involved, both on the Caribbean Basin Initiative. The Ford administration also compiled a 100 percent success rate on trade, but only two of these contested votes were on comprehensive trade measures. For more on the politics of trade, see I. M. Destler, *American Trade Politics* (Institute for International Economics and The Twentieth Century Fund, 1992).

[6] A January 14-17, 1995 Hart/Teeter poll conducted for NBC News and *The Wall Street Journal*, for example, asked respondents to name "the most important economic issue facing the country"; 32 percent named the federal budget deficit, compared to 27 percent for unemployment and percentages in the teens or lower for all other answers. The portion of respondents naming the deficit as the most serious economic problem has climbed steadily over recent years; it was 21 percent in 1991.

[7] *Budget of the United States, Fiscal Year 1996* (February, 1995). The FY1995 figure is based on estimates.

[8] Caroll J. Doherty, "Republicans Poised to Slash International Programs," *Congressional Quarterly* (May 13, 1995), pp. 1334-35.

Figure 1

Federal Budget Deficit at the End of Major Wars, 1916-1994

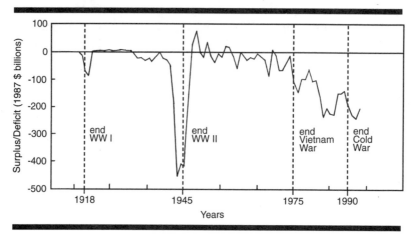

These deficit pressures transcend current shifts in partisan control. Each major war in this century led to higher deficits (see Figure 1). The Cold War has been no different. Some might argue that current deficits are a consequence of (depending on one's politics) the Reagan tax cuts or profligate domestic spending by Congress. Yet these are "war debts" as well, because they resulted in part from President Reagan's attempt to outgun and bankrupt the Soviets through a substantial arms build-up.

Today's deficits make many national security debates sound like the discussion aboard a life raft with a slow leak. The question is not what burdens to add next but which to jettison last. Even new initiatives are framed within fixed or declining budgets. The 1993 package of assistance to Russia and the other NIS is a good example: A sixfold increase in aid to these countries had to be squeezed within declining budget totals for foreign aid.[9] This

---

[9] The FY 1993 Foreign Operations appropriations bill totaled $26.26 billion; the FY 1994 bill totaled $12.98 billion. This decrease overstates the effective decline in foreign aid, however, for two reasons. First, $12.31 billion in the FY 1993 bill was for the U.S. quota for the International Monetary Fund, a periodic transaction that does not result in budget outlays or affect the U.S. budget deficit. Second, as noted in Chapter 2, the FY 1994 bill included $0.6 billion in supplemental FY 1993 Foreign Operations funds. Correcting for the IMF quota and counting the FY 1993 supple-

zero-sum politics of national security has applied to recent aid initiatives toward South Africa and other nations as well. Deficit imperatives also are constraining defense initiatives (although within a much larger budget), triggering an intense debate among the military services over what roles, missions, and weapons each will have within a stagnant or shrinking budget.

The high budget deficit and the more diffuse set of security threats have contributed to a more critical political tone toward international programs in general. In a press conference soon after the 1994 elections, Sen. Jesse Helms (R-NC) said: "The so-called foreign aid program...has spent an estimated $2 trillion of the American taxpayers' money, much of it going down foreign rat holes, to countries that constantly oppose us in the United Nations, and many of which reject concepts of freedom."[10] Republican Sen. Phil Gramm of Texas, announcing his 1996 presidential bid, said the U.S. foreign aid budget is like "a little rich kid in the middle of a slum with a cake," and suggested that the United States should "keep the cake" and instead share the "recipe" of free enterprise and personal freedom.

Pressures on international programs have come from both parties. In 1991, House Majority Whip David Bonior (D-MI) argued against a $1-billion aid package for the disintegrating Soviet Union, saying: "I don't think we should do anything for the Soviets until we take care of our own."[11] Similarly, even though President Clinton has argued against American withdrawal from international affairs, his 1992 campaign book pledged to cut the international affairs budget by $2 billion by "reforming" foreign aid.[12]

---

mental funds as part of the FY 1994 bill, the FY 1993 bill would have totaled $13.94 billion and the FY 1994 bill would have totaled $13.58—still a decrease. *Congressional Quarterly* (October 10, 1992), p. 3179; (October 2, 1993), p. 2660.

[10] John M. Goshko and Daniel Williams, "U.S. Policy Faces Review by Helms," *The Washington Post* (November 13, 1994), p. A1.

[11] *Congressional Quarterly Almanac: 102nd Congress, 1st Session, 1991* (Congressional Quarterly, 1992), p. 468.

[12] Gov. Bill Clinton and Sen. Al Gore, *Putting People First: How We Can All Change America* (Times Books, 1992), p. 30.

Changes in the Balance of Power

Many studies of the relationship between Congress and the executive branch on national security focus on the relative strength of the two branches and note the rise in congressional power after the Vietnam War. This line of analysis is problematic in many ways. For one, there is no accepted way to measure each branch's strength. Roll call votes only tell a part of the story. Presidents often act without seeking congressional support. When they do, it may indicate Congress is submissive and unlikely to object (Truman sending troops to Korea) or assertive and unlikely to approve (Clinton sending troops to Haiti).

Moreover, in many ways the competition over national security issues does not occur between the two branches so much as between opposing "issue networks."[13] Each of these networks cuts across not only the branches but also the public and private sectors, and may include congressional members and staff, executive branch bureaucrats, military officials, experts from think tanks and interest groups, business executives, and the media. Viewed from this cross-cutting perspective, the winner in each debate is not a branch but an issue position—sanctions on South Africa, for example, or production of the MX missile. The strength of each branch thus becomes a cumulative function of the positions a majority of its members adopt. In the cases that follow, there is much to support this analytical perspective.

Despite its limitations, though, analyzing the relative strength of the two branches remains valid and important. Each branch has distinct constitutional prerogatives and political assets. How well each branch mobilizes its resources shapes

---

[13] See, for example: Hugh Heclo, "Issue Networks and the Executive Establishment," in Anthony King, ed., *The New American Political System* (American Enterprise Institute, 1978), pp. 87-124. A question that deserves further inquiry is how the end of the Cold War is changing these networks. Some writers have asserted a trend toward more diverse and democratized participation in international affairs; for example: Ernest J. Wilson III, "Double Diversity: The Intersection of Big Changes at Home and Abroad," in Daniel Yankelovich and I. M. Destler, eds., *op. cit.*, pp. 154-74; Michael Clough, "Grass-Roots Policymaking: Say Good-Bye to the 'Wise Men,'" *Foreign Affairs* (January/February 1994), pp. 2-7. More analysis is required to determine the extent of such changes and their impact on national security policy.

Figure 2

Presidential Success Rates on Contested National Security Votes, 1974–1994

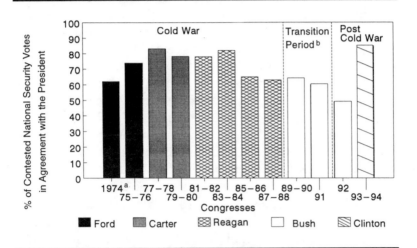

a The second session of the 93rd Congress is shown separately because Gerald Ford became President in the middle of the 93rd Congress.

b The two years of the 102nd Congress of 1991–92 are separated to show the change at the start of the post-Cold War period, as defined by this study.

much in the conduct of U.S. national security policy. The most striking changes amount to a paradox: the post-Cold War White House seems to be getting stronger on national security in some ways, while Congress seems increasingly assertive in others.

Nothing illustrates this paradox as well as the success rates of the Bush and Clinton administrations on contested national security votes. In 1992, the Bush administration prevailed on only 49 percent of contested national security votes, the lowest rate of any administration since the end of the Vietnam War (see Figure 2). One or both chambers of Congress voted against the administration on such major issues as China's trade status, defense spending levels, and nuclear testing. Yet Congress sustained the Clinton administration's position on 85 percent of contested votes in the 103rd Congress—the *highest* post-Vietnam rate—approving most of the administration's top priorities, including NAFTA, the new

GATT agreement, expansion of aid to Russia and the NIS, and defeating the vast majority of amendments proposing cuts to the administration's defense budget.

Democratic control of both branches from 1993-94 surely explains much of the difference between the two presidents' success rates. Yet even this partisan factor cannot explain the paradox, since Clinton's record on contested national security votes was higher than that of President Carter, who also enjoyed a Congress controlled by his party, while President Bush's 1992 success rate was lower than that of President Reagan in 1987-88, when he also faced a House and Senate controlled by Democrats.

Congress's activities on war powers paint another paradoxical picture. The War Powers Resolution, passed in 1973 over President Nixon's veto, has had a troubled life; it is debatable whether it ever has curtailed presidential decisions about the use of force abroad. Even so, the act was often the rhetorical rallying point for Congress's attempts to rein in foreign interventions. Since the end of the Cold War, however, and especially after the Gulf War, members of Congress have only infrequently invoked the Resolution in arguing against foreign interventions. By 1994, even the Resolution's supporters were declaring it a "dead letter"; in 1995, the new Senate Republican Majority Leader, Sen. Robert Dole (R-KS), introduced legislation to repeal the key provisions of the Resolution, and the House came within 16 votes of adopting such a measure.[14]

At the same time, Congress has become *more* energetic in asserting its war powers through other means.[15] Even as it was allowing the War Powers Resolution to fade from debate, Congress cut off funding for the U.S. troop presence in Somalia and Rwanda—the first times it had used the power of the purse to shut down an American military operation since the Vietnam era. Congress also declined to authorize the president's deployment of U.S. troops to Haiti, and it imposed a series of policy and funding restrictions on U.S. involvement in peacekeeping. Moreover, the

---

[14] Rep. Howard Berman, *Congressional Record* (October 6, 1994), p. H 11116.

[15] See James M. Lindsay, "Congress and the Use of Force in the Post-Cold War Era," Revised version of paper presented at the Aspen Strategy Group Conference, "The United States and the Use of Force in the Post-Cold War Era," August 1994.

balanced budget amendment narrowly defeated in March 1995 contained language that could well have strengthened Congress's role in war powers debates with the executive branch.[16]

It is tempting to conclude from this mixed picture that there is no clear post-Cold War trend in executive-congressional relations, or that presidential wins and losses in Congress are simply a function of partisan divisions, the competence of an administration's handling of Congress, and presidential popularity at the time of the vote. While each of these factors is important, this study concludes that the mixed picture in executive-congressional relations reflects two different groups of national security challenges. Congress is becoming more assertive on non-traditional security challenges, such as peacekeeping, on which the security stakes for the U.S. are not high or not widely accepted. But there has been little decline in executive branch power on "traditional" security issues, such as defense spending and great power relations.

Partisan balances between the two branches will change this picture in predictable ways. When one party controls both branches, as during 1993-94, Congress will be relatively less powerful on national security; when control is split between the two parties, as it was from 1987 to 1992, and as it has been since 1995, Congress will be relatively more powerful. The impact of partisan shifts on the relative power of each branch is revealed by the Clinton administration's veto threats on national security legislation: none during the entire 103rd Congress; two in just the first five months of the 104th Congress. Yet even as partisan control changes, it is likely that the balance of power between the two branches on national security policy will continue to offer a mixed picture, and the White House position will be more likely to prevail on traditional than non-traditional security issues.

---

[16] The versions of the amendment voted on in 1994 and narrowly defeated by the Senate in early March 1995 both included this language: "The provisions of this article may be waived for any fiscal year in which the United States is engaged in military conflict which causes an imminent and serious military threat to national security *and is so declared by a joint resolution, adopted by a majority of the whole number of each house, which becomes law*" [emphasis added]. This language would have required the executive branch to obtain congressional action, if not authorization, on any military deployment that it wished to finance by running a deficit. I am indebted to Thomas Mann for highlighting this implication of the amendment.

Institutional and Partisan Changes

The end of the Cold War also has brought institutional and partisan changes in the relationship between Congress and the executive—that is, changes in how the two branches are organized and who controls them.

The most dramatic change right now is the Republican takeover of the Congress for the first time in 40 years. While the 1994 congressional campaigns were waged almost exclusively over domestic matters, the change of partisan control will have sweeping implications for Congress's activities on national security policy. There are new chairmen for every one of the committees that work on defense, trade, and foreign policy, and in a few cases—such as the replacement of Sen. Claiborne Pell (D-RI) as chair of the Senate Foreign Relations Committee with Sen. Helms—the differences could not be more extreme. The Republicans have staked out several issues on which they differ with Democrats in Congress and the White House. These include:

- *Peacekeeping.* Both the House GOP's Contract with America and new legislation proposed by Senate Majority Leader Dole call for restrictions on peacekeeping funding and missions. At this writing, the House has adopted most of the peacekeeping provisions in the Contract, including measures that would significantly reduce U.S. payments for UN peacekeeping operations—provisions the White House has opposed and suggested it would veto.

- *Defense spending.* The Contract also criticized the Clinton administration's cuts in defense spending and proposed a panel to examine possible increases. Leading Republican defense legislators, such as Sens. John McCain (R-AZ) and John Warner (R-VA), have criticized the Clinton defense budgets for including high levels of non-traditional defense expenditures and producing low levels of readiness to fight and win two major regional conflicts. However, the Republican Party's "defense hawks" are colliding with its "deficit hawks," just as they did in 1994. Republican deficit hawks joined Democrats in late February 1995 to defeat a provision within the Contract with America supporting a national missile defense system.[17] Speaker of the House Newt Gingrich (R-GA) reflected this conflict by declaring his intent to be a "cheap hawk."[18]

- **Foreign aid.** Several of the new Republican chairmen of national security committees have criticized foreign aid in general terms and called for specific funding cuts. In addition to Sen. Helms's derision of foreign aid as "rat hole" spending, Sen. McConnell, chair of the Senate subcommittee that funds foreign aid, proposed cutting most foreign aid accounts by 20 percent.[19] Republicans have suggested that programs on population, the global environment, Africa, and humanitarian relief are the most likely to be cut.

- **Russia.** Several key Republicans have criticized the Clinton administration for adopting a "Russia-first" policy among the former Soviet states and have proposed a more confrontational tone with Moscow.[20] Combined with the critical reaction to Russia's military campaign in Chechnya, this view has prompted calls by Republicans to cut or restrict aid to Russia and to extend NATO membership more quickly to certain Central European nations, notably the Czech Republic, Hungary, Poland, and Slovakia.

---

[17] It is also noteworthy that one of the only significant reductions Congress has made to the Clinton defense budgets was imposed as part of the 1994 (FY 1995) budget resolution due to an amendment to the resolution in the Budget Committee sponsored by Sens. James Exon (D-NE) and Charles Grassley (R-IA); the amendment called for $26 billion cut over five years in all discretionary accounts, including defense. The committee vote was 13-8, with all nine of the panel's Republicans voting in favor. George Hager, "Senate Panel's Spending Plan Includes More Deficit Cuts," *Congressional Quarterly* (March 19, 1994), pp. 655-56.

[18] Bill Gertz, "Gingrich Eyes Aid Cutoff if Russia Deals with Iran," *The Washington Times* (February 22, 1995), p. A12.

[19] In his December 12, 1994 press conference, McConnell offered an outline for the FY 1996 foreign operations appropriations bill that would cut foreign aid by about 10 percent overall. However, since several large aid recipients, such as Israel and Egypt, would be "held harmless," McConnell predicted cuts of about 20 percent for "everybody outside of the Middle East and Europe." Federal News Service transcript.

[20] Carla Anne Robbins, "Kentucky Senator, Handed Keys to Foreign Aid, to be Most Potent Foe of Clinton's Russia Policy," *The Wall Street Journal* (December 13, 1994), p. A20. Similarly, a top aide to Senate Foreign Relations chairman Helms suggested that the United States replace the policy of containing Russia with a policy of "encircling" Russia. Saul Friedman, "A Chill in Foreign Policy Arena," *Newsday* (November 20, 1994), p. 19.

- *Bosnia*. One of the first bills introduced in the new Congress by Senate Majority Leader Dole was a measure he had sponsored in the previous Congress, along with Democratic Senator Joseph Lieberman (CT), to force a unilateral lifting of the arms embargo on Bosnia. While some key Republicans, such as former Secretary of State James Baker and Sen. Warner, have dissented, Dole's policy consistently attracted the support of at least 70 percent of congressional Republicans throughout the 103rd Congress and accounted for four of the ten cases in which the Clinton administration lost contested votes in Congress.

Presidential politics sharpen the differences across the aisle. National security credentials play an important substantive and symbolic role in the quadrennial race among would-be commanders-in-chief. Just as past Democratic Congresses used foreign policy issues to boost their party's presidential prospects, today's Republican Party leaders and members of Congress, including the four Republican senators and one Republican House member planning to run in 1996—Sens. Dole, Gramm (TX), Lugar (IN), and Specter (PA), and Rep. Dornan (CA)—clearly see electoral advantages in criticizing the Clinton foreign policy record.

The partisan change in Congress affects not only issues but also institutions. Many national security bureaus and agencies had developed close working relations with the key members of the Democratic majority. When the Clinton administration during its first months considered folding the Arms Control and Disarmament Agency into the State Department, for example, ACDA was able to count on several key members and congressional staffers to derail the proposal. The foreign policy agencies tend to have weaker ties to the new Republican majority. Partly as a result, bills now advancing to floor votes in both the House and the Senate would eliminate not only ACDA, but also the Agency for International Development and the U.S. Information Agency.

Some observers have suggested the new Congress and its Republican majority are "isolationist." This is too strong, at least by historical standards. World War II and the Cold War relegated the isolationism of the 1920s and 1930s to the fringes of American political discourse.[21] Moreover, many members of the Republican leadership have played key roles in supporting U.S. programs abroad; as Chapter 2 makes clear, Speaker Gingrich and other Republican leaders helped ensure passage of the 1993 Russia/NIS assistance package. Even so, the statements of Republican leaders and rank and file alike suggest the Party's center of gravity is moving away from international programs. While the result may not be an active choice of isolation so much as a passive, budget-driven drift toward indifference, leaders in both parties nonetheless must choose how much political capital to spend in countering this trend. The choice is especially important for the Republican Party: having tipped the political scales toward isolationism during the 1930s and internationalism during the Cold War era, it holds the balance of power once again.

As historic as the Republican ascendancy in Congress is, it is not the only important partisan or institutional change in national security relations between the two branches. Indeed, other post-Cold War changes will have an offsetting or longer-lasting influence.

For example, while the end of the Cold War brought the first Republican Congress in 40 years, it also brought the first Democratic White House in 12 years. There was much continuity between the foreign policies of the Bush and Clinton administrations, particularly on trade liberalization, the Mideast peace process, and willingness to use force to contain Iraq. Yet the Clinton administration also brought distinct policy changes, including expanded aid to former Soviet states, stronger support for peacekeeping and humanitarian missions such as in Haiti, an expanded agenda for non-proliferation and arms control, and a quicker pace of force reductions in the U.S. military. The Clinton administration also introduced some minor but notable changes in the organization of the executive branch on national security issues—particularly the creation of a National Economic Council

---

[21] Recent polls suggest the public also has not turned isolationist. For example, a Chicago Council on Foreign Relations poll conducted in late 1994 finds that 65 percent of the public wants the U.S. to play an "active role" in world affairs — slightly higher than in 1986 (64 percent) or 1990 (62 percent) and significantly higher than in 1982 (54 percent). *American Public Opinion and U.S. Foreign Policy 1995* (Chicago Council on Foreign Relations, 1995), p.13.

Figure 3

Turnover of Partisan Control of the Presidency, Senate, and House, 1917–1995

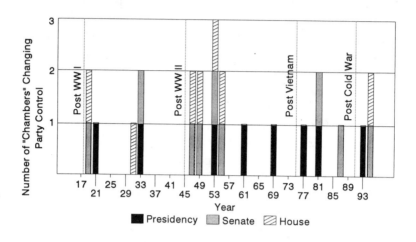

to centralize and coordinate economic policymaking at the White House.

It is not at all paradoxical that the end of the Cold War moved Congress toward the Republican right even as it moved the White House in the opposite direction. The common element is the rejection of incumbents. This phenomenon, which was so vivid in 1994, has been the norm after major wars throughout this century (see Figure 3). The Democrats lost their majorities in the House and Senate in 1918 as World War I ended, and they lost the White House two years later. The Democrats lost control of Congress again the year after World War II ended, and they came close to losing the presidency as well in 1948. The Republican sweep of both branches in 1952 was partly a reaction to the Korean War. And the Republicans lost the White House after the Vietnam War (although Watergate clearly was a major factor). There are examples of the pattern abroad as well, such as Great Britain's rejection of Winston Churchill and the Tories after World War II. The connecting thread is the public's desire for change

Figure 4

Number of New Members Elected to U.S. House of Representatives, 1916–1994

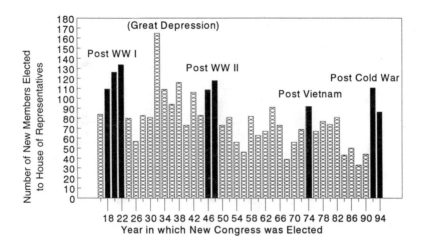

and prosperity after the sacrifices of the war years— and, in some cases, the public's rejection of one party for its prosecution of the war.[22]

In the same way, the popular dissatisfaction that swept both the Bush administration and the congressional Democrats out of power flowed in part from a sense among voters that domestic conditions ought to be improving more quickly now that the Cold War is over. For example, during the 1992 campaign, Gov. Clinton said: "All around the world, the American Dream—political freedom, market economics, national independence—is ascendant.... Yet we're not celebrating. Why? Because our people fear that while the American Dream reigns supreme abroad, it is dying here at home."[23]   It

---

[22] See Ornstein, *op. cit.*, p. 109. The point here is not that economic and domestic issues become subsidiary in postwar elections; only that the war affects the domestic economy and changes how voters factor in domestic issues in general.

[23] "The New Covenant: Responsibility and Rebuilding the American Community," Address at Georgetown University, October 23, 1991.

Figure 5

Votes by Non-Freshmen and Freshmen in Support of Administration Position on Contested Trade Votes, Senate and House, 103rd Congress (1993–94)

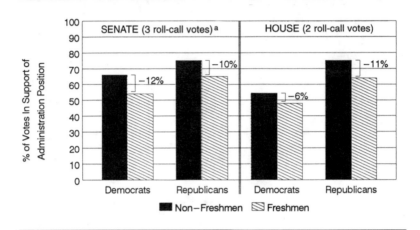

[a] Sen. Shelby was counted as a Democrat on the NAFTA vote and as a Republican on the GATT votes.

remains unclear, of course, whether the electorate's postwar restiveness will now result in a continuing propensity to "throw the rascals out," or, as some contend, in a long-term Republican majority in Congress and perhaps in the White House as well.

An important implication of the high rates of political turnover since the end of the Cold War is the large number of freshmen elected to Congress. The 1992 elections brought 110 freshmen to the House and 11 to the Senate; 1994 brought 86 House freshmen and another 11 new senators. As a result, over half of current House members have been elected since the fall of the Berlin Wall. This is the largest influx of new members since the elections of 1946 and 1948. This influx of newcomers, too, is typical after the conclusion of major wars (see Figure 4).

Although virtually all of the new members campaigned on domestic issues, their arrival promises to influence U.S. national security policy significantly in the coming years. Recent freshmen tend to vote differently on national security issues from their more experienced colleagues, even accounting for partisan differences.

Figures 5 through 9 show the differences in voting between fresh-men and non-freshmen on contested national security votes in the 103rd Congress. Figure 5 suggests that freshmen were markedly less supportive of free trade agreements (NAFTA and GATT) than non-freshmen in their own parties. Figures 6 and 7 show a mixed picture for overall votes on foreign policy and defense. But when the analysis is narrowed to votes on foreign *spending* and defense *spending*, the freshmen once again vote in a distinctly different way. Figures 8 and 9 show the contrast for those contested votes on amendments proposing specific increases or decreases in for-eign or defense spending, such as amendments to delete funding for a weapons system. Figure 8 shows freshmen were less sup-portive of foreign spending than non-freshmen in their own party. Figure 9 suggests the freshmen more *polarized* on defense spend-ing, with freshmen Democrats less supportive of defense spending and freshmen Republicans more supportive of defense spending than non-freshmen in their own parties. This last finding suggests that, notwithstanding their reputation as deficit hawks, recent Republican freshmen are even more strongly *defense* hawks.

The distinctiveness of the freshmen on foreign policy was evi-dent during the opening days of the 104th Congress. At the first hearing of the House Committee on International Relations, the chairman and ranking Democrat convened the session with pleas-ant, non-partisan remarks. The first freshman to speak, Rep. David Funderburk (R-NC), struck quite a different tone, launching into a biting, partisan attack on the Clinton administration's for-eign policy. Freshmen also played a visible role in Congress's reaction to the Mexican peso crisis, as will be discussed in Chapter 4. That case and others suggest that today's freshmen feel relatively free to buck their party elders—even Rep. Gingrich, who is proving himself the most influential Speaker in decades.

There are several reasons why today's congressional freshmen have different views on national security than their colleagues. For a start, they are younger than their non-freshmen colleagues; 56 percent of the freshmen of the 104th Congress are under age 45, compared to 17 percent of the non-freshmen. The freshmen also have far less military experience: a decade ago, at least 56 percent of House members were military veterans; now the fig-ure is 40 percent; among the freshmen of the 103rd and 104th

Figure 6

Votes by Non-Freshmen and Freshmen in Support of Administration Position on Contested Foreign Policy Votes, Senate and House, 103rd Congress (1993–94)

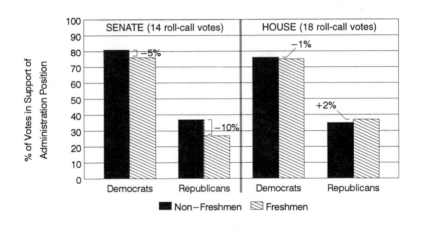

Figure 7

Votes by Non-Freshmen and Freshmen in Support of Administration Position on Contested Defense Votes, Senate and House, 103rd Congress (1993–94)

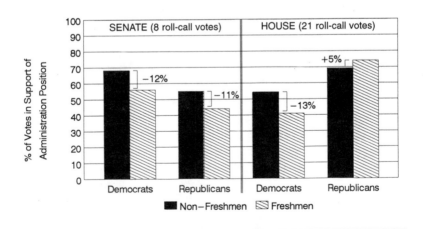

Figure 8

Votes by Non-Freshmen and Freshmen in Support of Administration Position on Contested Foreign Policy Spending Votes, Senate and House, 103rd Congress (1993–94)

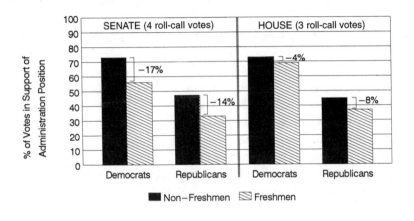

Figure 9

Votes by Non-Freshmen and Freshmen in Support of Administration Position on Contested Defense Spending Votes, Senate and House, 103rd Congress (1993–94)

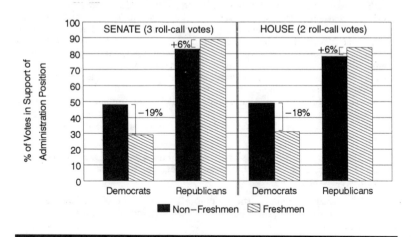

Congresses, the figure is about 20 percent.[24] The military experience of the non-freshmen may give them more grounding in not
only the defense budget but also on many aspects of trade and foreign policy.[25] More generally, the post-Cold War newcomers as a
group reflect the heightened public concern over deficits and the
reduced concern over national security that prevailed at the time
of their election.[26]

The end of the Cold War has not yet brought major restruc-
turings of Congress's processes for acting on national security.
The new Republican House gave the Foreign Affairs and Armed
Services committees the new names of "International Relations"
and "National Security," respectively, but did not alter their jurisdiction significantly.[27] The foreign policy authorizing committees are notably weak relative to the appropriations committees,
but the decline of the former—especially that of the once-power-
ful Senate Foreign Relations Committee—began decades ago.
While not a result of restructuring, the increased concern over

---

[24] The percentage for the Congress elected in 1984 is based on biographical
information in *Politics in America, 1985* (Congressional Quarterly Press, 1984);
this information may not provide an exhaustive accounting for members with military service. In the 103rd and 104th Congresses, 20 percent and 22 percent of all
members, respectively, had military service; unpublished data courtesy of
Congressional Quarterly, Inc.

[25] One example of the link between members' military service and their
views on national security comes from Rep. Sam Gibbons (D-FL), the only sitting
member of the House to land at Normandy on D-Day, and now ranking Democrat
on the International Trade subcommittee of the Ways and Means committee. His
narrative of his D-Day experience suggests that it fostered his interest in international trade: "World commerce had been destroyed by an act of Congress in the
Smoot-Hawley Tariff. . . . A feeling of despair swept Europe and Japan. . . . These
events and my own experiences long ago gave me a mission . . . to help create an
environment in which people can work and live together—not just in the United
States, but worldwide. The opportunity to create a peaceful environment with
our political differences is not very good, but in our commercial contacts we can
build confidence, understanding and a spirit of cooperation. So my mission is to
do that." Sam Gibbons, "June 6, 1944—I Was There," unpublished memoir dic-
tated in 1980, p. 19-20.

[26] This kind of cohort effect has been noted for earlier influxes of freshmen,
such as the class elected in 1974; see: Burdett Loomis, *The New American
Politician* (Basic Books, 1988).

[27] The House did change the subcommittee structure of the International
Security Committee and expanded its jurisdiction to include some aspects of the
merchant marine.

economic issues and the declining power of the foreign policy committees has helped strengthen the voice in national security debates of committees whose main focus is not national security—such as the work of the tax committees on international trade agreements or the focus of the Senate Energy Committee on the North Korean nuclear agreement.[28] The new Republican majority has committed itself to reduce congressional staffs significantly, and it already has eliminated the budget for the House Foreign Policy and Arms Control Caucus, along with those for other issue caucuses. Although the increase in congressional staff in the 1960s and 1970s is often cited as having contributed to Congress's rise in influence, it is too early to assess the effects of the new staff cuts.

The Postwar Pattern

In attempting to understand this collection of changes—which do not at first blush clearly suggest that Congress has grown either weaker or stronger relative to the executive—we should start with the recognition, noted by others, that the relationship between the White House and Capitol Hill tends to change dramatically after major wars.[29] This historical pattern is hardly surprising. One aim of war is to change the international security environment; America's major wars almost always have. A large shift in the security environment changes the national security dialogue between the two branches. Moreover, wars are pivotal political events. They reshape public opinion—of the world, of America's

---

[28] Ornstein, "Congress in the Post-Cold War World," op. cit., p. 114.

[29] See, for example, Arthur Schlesinger's The Imperial Presidency (Houghton Mifflin, 1973), which traces changes in the war powers relation after major wars; or Franck and Weisband, op. cit. Similarly, James Lindsay, op. cit, organizes his overview of the executive-congressional relationship roughly around periods defined by the major wars. Blechman and Mann, op. cit., both focus on changes in the relationship that followed the end of the Vietnam War. This study considers the "major" American wars of this century to be World War I, World War II, and Vietnam. This list excludes many significant conflicts, particularly the Korean and Gulf wars. These have been excluded because America's involvement was relatively brief and did not entail as high a cost in dollars and casualties as the other three. As noted in the text, however, at least some of the patterns discussed here also held true for the Korean conflict.

purposes and security needs, and of how well each of the two branches' leaders have worked to meet those needs. Wars also influence the domestic economy, usually driving up employment, inflation, and deficits while the battle rages, and often triggering recessions after the fighting stops. These economic consequences also affect the political environment.

A quick survey of the executive-congressional relationship after the century's major wars makes this pattern clear (although the following glosses over the numerous exceptions and variations to the general rule).[30] Prior to World War I, Congress played a limited role in foreign policy by modern standards, with much of its influence exerted by rejecting foreign treaties, especially in the late 1800s. After the Armistice, however, the postwar Congresses showed an even greater determination to resist White House activism abroad. Congress rejected the Treaty of Versailles and the League of Nations in three successive Senate votes, entered a period of relative quiescence during the 1920s while Republicans controlled both branches, and then reasserted itself as the nation entered the 1930s. Congress passed the notorious Smoot-Hawley tariffs in 1930, rejected the treaty creating the World Court in 1935, worked to strengthen the neutrality acts, and even as late as 1941 passed by only a one-vote margin a measure to extend the length of service for military draftees.

After World War II, and in good part because of it, the executive emerged far stronger and became increasingly dominant as the years passed. President Truman, working closely with Senator Vandenberg and other Republicans, was able to get the North Atlantic Treaty ratified. He turned back attempts in the Senate's "Great Debate" of 1951 to withdraw U.S. troops from Europe. He introduced American troops into Korea without first notifying Congress—and without major congressional objection. When President Eisenhower asked Congress to authorize his deployment of troops to Formosa, Congress obliged with nearly unanimous votes. Congress played virtually no role in the Kennedy administration's decision to launch the Bay of Pigs operation, to

---

[30] This historical overview draws heavily on Schlesinger, *op. cit.*; Lindsay, *op. cit.*, pp. 14-29; and Blechman, *op. cit.*, pp. 3-22.

impose a naval quarantine on Cuba, or to increase the number of U.S advisers in Vietnam. Congress passed the Tonkin Gulf Resolution with only two dissenting votes.

The Vietnam War ended this era of congressional quiescence. Spurred by sharp increases in public sentiment against the war, Congress in the 1970s asserted its national security prerogatives more than ever before. It passed the War Powers Resolution over President Nixon's veto in 1973. It cut off funds for the war. It imposed an arms embargo on Turkey. It began reviewing arms sales, weapons systems, and covert intelligence operations. It forced President Carter to put the SALT II nuclear treaty on hold, but also became increasingly active in pushing for nuclear arms control measures, such as the nuclear freeze. This congressional activism continued in varying degrees through the 1980s.

The war that has recently ended was of course different from the century's others. For most of its years, the Cold War was an armed standoff rather than an armed conflict. During its later years, it was not even supported by a military draft. Yet the Cold War was a major war in many of the ways that affect executive-congressional relations. It mobilized the United States against the threat of a foreign adversary. It elevated defense spending, the importance of the armed forces, and the president's role as commander-in-chief. As with the earlier wars, therefore, we should expect the conclusion of the Cold War to change executive-congressional relations on national security again. But do the changes we are seeing today and the changes that followed the century's earlier wars fit into some kind of a pattern?

Shifts in the Tug-of-War

Schlesinger writes of "the postwar congressional impulse to strike back at the war-magnified presidency."[31] That impulse, however, has been stronger or weaker after different wars. A look at the century's major conflicts suggests at least four factors that appear to predict the degree of the relative changes in power between the two branches after a war. In descending order of importance, they

---

[31] Schlesinger, *op. cit.*, p. 127.

are: 1) perceptions of security threats after the war; 2) perceptions of the war just ended; 3) the state of the economy after the war; and 4) the way in which the executive branch manages its relations with Congress on national security issues, particularly whether it reaches out to both parties in Congress. Applied to the current, post-Cold War period, the factors point in different directions—that is, they suggest Congress should be stronger in some ways and weaker in others. This is exactly what we are seeing.

Did the two branches agree on the nature and severity of the new security threat? In the new security environment that follows a war, one of the central challenges of political leadership is to define what security threats should concern the nation. The degree to which a president convinces the Congress and the public in the years following a war that a distinct and severe security threat exists appears to be the single most important determinant of the executive's relative strength with Congress on national security issues. As I. M. Destler has noted, "crisis usually reinforces presidential power and the argument that the president needs the flexibility to respond."[32] The complex dynamics of world affairs rarely define themselves as a crisis, however, and in the period immediately following a war it takes particular effort for a president to convince the public and Congress that the nation faces a new, long-term threat.

After World War I, President Wilson went to Congress to promote the Treaty of Versailles and the League of Nations. The justification he provided was not only idealistic but vague: "It was our duty to do everything that it was within our power to do to make the triumph of freedom and of right a lasting triumph in the assurance of which men might everywhere live without fear. . . . It was universally recognized that all the peoples of the world demanded of the Conference that it should create such a continuing concert of free nations as would make wars of aggression and spoliation such as this that has just ended forever impossible."[33]

---

[32] I. M. Destler, "Executive-Congressional Conflict in Foreign Policy: Explaining It, Coping With It," in Lawrence C. Dodd and Bruce I. Oppenheimer, eds., *Congress Reconsidered* (Congressional Quarterly Press, 1985), p. 344.

[33] Woodrow Wilson, Address to the Senate Presenting the Peace Treaty, July 10, 1919, *Presidential Messages, Addresses and State Papers*, pp. 698-712.

The Senate did not hear in this language any threat that justified the loss of sovereignty implicit in membership in the League.

After World War II, in contrast, President Truman was able to persuade Congress that communist expansion constituted a clear and present danger. In March 1947, in response to the events in Greece and Turkey, he convened a joint session of Congress and began with these words: "The gravity of the situation which confronts the world today necessitates my appearance before a joint session of the Congress. The foreign policy and the national security of this country are involved."[34] The choice of venue and words were directly tied to executive-congressional relations, as is clear from this account of a meeting just days before Truman's address:

> . . . Congressional leaders were soon summoned to smooth the way for quick passage of the bill [responding to the Greek-Turkish crisis]. Secretary Marshall took the lead in explaining the situation. With his mind on the poverty that was so powerfully an ally of the Cummunists in Greece, the Secretary emphasized the need for economic relief. The Republican leaders stirred irritably. Did this Administration really expect the Congress of Robert Taft to play WPA to the Greeks? Undersecretary of State Dean Acheson, sensing trouble, turned to President Truman and asked if he might add some remarks. Acheson said little about economic distress. Instead he moved over to the big wall map with pointer in hand and described in detail just what strategic consequences would follow the fall of Greece to Red armies. The Republican leaders began relaxing. . . . As Vandenberg left, he remarked to Truman, "Mr. President, if thats what you want, there's only one way to get it. That is to make a personal appearance before Congress and scare hell out of the country."[35]

The story reminds us that Congress yields to the executive in the face of strategic threats far more readily than for humanitarian concerns. The case Truman made, and the factual evidence of Soviet expansionist aims, were enough to tip the balance of executive-congressional power for decades.

---

[34] Harry Truman, Address to a Joint Session of Congress, March 12, 1947.

[35] Eric F. Goldman, "The Crucial Decade—and After: America, 1945-1969 (Knopf,1971), p. 59.

After Vietnam, congressional leaders still largely agreed on the strategic threat posed by the Soviet Union and its nuclear arsenals. But the Vietnam War had left bitter divisions over the tactics the United States should pursue in countering the Soviets—divisions over détente versus confrontation; divisions over the right weapons systems and the right level of defense spending; divisions over how much the United States should view third world conflicts through an East-West lens. These tactical disagreements fueled the resurgence of congressional assertiveness.

Yet the degree of post-Vietnam congressional assertiveness was uneven (see Figure 2). During the early 1980s, the White House got its way more often on key national security votes. Part of this increase was no doubt due to the fact that President Reagan's own party controlled the Senate and often had a working majority in the House. But the increase also reflected concerns about a "hollow army" and "the window of vulnerability" in the nuclear balance and President Reagan's arms build-up during what has been called the "new Cold War."[36] As Mikhail Gorbachev embarked on *glasnost* and *perestroika* in the late 1980s and the United States perceived a less threatening Soviet Union, congressional assertiveness once again climbed. In other words, congressional assertiveness after Vietnam was stronger or weaker depending in part on perceptions of the Soviet threat.

Since the end of the Cold War, there has been a low level of agreement on the nature of the new security environment. Neither President Bush nor President Clinton has forged a consensus regarding an overriding strategic threat. Instead, both post-Cold War administrations have focused on a list of diverse security concerns—from the proliferation of weapons of mass destruction, to regional stability in the Mideast and Asia, to scattered humanitarian crises. With no agreement on America's overall security strategy, congressional relations have depended on Congress's assessment of the national security stakes in each vote, as the following chapters make clear. On issues where Congress perceives the security stakes to be low, such as peacekeeping, Congress has pressed its views forcefully. On issues

---

36 A. W. DePorte, *Europe Between the Superpowers: The Enduring Balance* (Yale University Press, 1986), p. 219.

where Congress is convinced America's security is at stake, as on the bills for aid to Russia and the other NIS in 1992 and 1993, the executive branch appears to remain at least as strong as it was during the post-Vietnam era.

As in 1947, congressional perceptions of a single issue may change depending on whether or not the challenge at hand is credibly framed in strategic terms. In 1991, then-Rep. Les Aspin and Sen. Sam Nunn proposed authorizing $1 billion for the disintegrating Soviet Union, mostly as a humanitarian initiative. The proposal was dropped for lack of White House and congressional support. At the end of the year, it was repackaged as a $500-million program, mostly for dismantling Soviet nuclear weapons. Congress passed it.[37] This is not to say that executive branch officials who want congressional support for a humanitarian initiative should simply dress it up in strategic clothing. Recent efforts by some writers and officials to portray the problems of failed states, overpopulation, environmental degradation, and migration as adding up to a strategic threat of global "chaos" appear to have changed few minds in Congress, particularly among moderate and conservative members.[38]

Congressional and public perceptions of the nation's external threats will continue to be the most important factor in relations between the branches on national security. As long as it continues, today's general lack of consensus on America's security threats will tend to strengthen Congress's hand in national security relative to the executive. If more serious threats emerge, or if an administration can paint today's diverse security challenges into one, compelling picture, the relative power of the executive will tend to increase.

---

[37] *Congressional Quarterly Almanac, 1991, op. cit.,* p. 106-H.

[38] See Robert D. Kaplan, "The Coming Anarchy," *Atlantic Monthly* (February, 1994), pp. 44-76.; Matthew Connelly and Paul Kennedy, "Must it be the Rest Against the West?" *The Atlantic Monthly* (December, 1994), pp. 61-84; Undersecretary of State Timothy Wirth, National Press Club Luncheon address, July 12, 1994; Agency for International Development Administrator Brian Atwood, "Suddenly, Chaos," *The Washington Post* (July 31, 1994), p. C9. For a critique of this thesis and its political impact, see: Jeremy D. Rosner, "Is Chaos America's Real Enemy?" *The Washington Post* (August 14, 1994), P. C1; and Jeremy D. Rosner, "The Sources of Chaos," *The New Democrat* (November 1994), pp. 20-22.

What are perceptions of the war that just ended and the role each branch played? The executive branch tends to emerge stronger in its post-war relations with Congress if the public and Congress perceive the war as justified and successful. Despite the Allied victory, World War I left the nation with a bitter aftertaste. Political debates were filled with charges that the United States had been drawn into a European problem and that arms merchants had profiteered off the conflict. These perceptions strengthened Congress's hand against President Wilson's postwar international activism. World War II, in contrast, was seen as both necessary and effective. Because the executive had long argued for American involvement while Congress had been a holdout, the executive came away stronger in its national security relations with Congress. By the late 1960s, Vietnam was increasingly seen as unwise and unsuccessful. Congress's hand was strengthened as its members made the dubious case that the war had been the executive branch's responsibility—that Congress had been drawn into the quagmire unwittingly—and as President Nixon defied Congress's efforts to stop America's involvement in the conflict.

The Cold War is overwhelmingly perceived as having been justified and successful. When President Bush announced to Congress and the nation that, "by the grace of God, America has won the Cold War," there was thunderous applause and not a peep of disagreement.[39] A successful war generally would strengthen the executive's hand relative to the Congress. Yet, unlike after World War II (the last major war that was broadly seen as justified and successful), there is little perception that one branch was more responsible for winning the conflict than the other. Thus, the positive perception of the Cold War effort is less likely to change the balance of power between the two branches on national security.

What is more important are the lessons that political leaders have drawn from the Cold War and how they apply them to current challenges. Unlike past wars, there was no single moment, like D-Day, when the tide of battle in the Cold War turned. Competing explanations regarding the Cold War's end focus on the Reagan defense build-up, Western efforts to promote human

---

[39] State of the Union address, January 28, 1992.

rights behind the Iron Curtain, or the Soviet empire's own economic and political failures in the face of a new global economy. The relative strengths of these explanations have important consequences for post-Cold War discussions between Congress and the White House. For example, those who champion the second view tended to oppose renewing China's most-favored-nation trade status after the Tiananmen massacre, while those who hold the third view tended to support unlinking China's trade status from its human rights record.

Generally, popular perceptions of the Cold War tend to increase the strength of the executive branch on national security programs that played some role in the West's victory. The defense budget, intelligence operations, and democracy promotion programs, among others, all can claim to have speeded the Cold War's end, and all have fared well in recent congressional votes.[40] By contrast, peacekeeping operations, global environmental protection, and population programs played virtually no role in ending the Cold War, and each of these has been divisive in congressional-executive relations.

What is the condition of the U.S. economy after the war? The conclusion of a war typically leads to economic contraction, displacement, and anxiety as demand for defense materiel declines, troops return to civilian work, and the public refocuses on domestic matters. The impact of U.S. economic conditions on congressional attitudes toward national security is complex. It is beyond the scope of this study to trace all the connections after each major war in the century. We can at least hypothesize, however, that harsher than anticipated economic conditions after a war make Congress more resistant to executive leadership on national security initiatives.

The experience after World War I provides mixed evidence for this thesis. The Senate rejected the Treaty of Versailles in 1919 during a brief postwar economic surge. Yet the year had opened with a recession, and even as the recovery proceeded, there was concern that this boomlet was built atop speculation and war

---

[40] For example, both President Clinton and President Bush prevailed on contested votes significantly more on defense than on foreign policy—89 percent compared to 78 percent for Clinton, and 70 percent compared to 45 percent for Bush.

debts.[41] Those concerns were soon proven correct. The economy went into a steep recession in 1920-21; unemployment remained at more than twice the prewar level for a full three years. These conditions helped fuel the yearning for a return to "normalcy," the Republican victories in 1920, and Congress's lack of appetite for international activism throughout the decade. The crash of 1929 and the Great Depression that followed further stiffened Congress's resolve against foreign commitments, even as Roosevelt started forecasting Europe's gathering storm.

The contraction immediately after World War II was deeper than that of 1920, but it ended more quickly than many observers had expected. The GNP contracted by 19 percent in real terms in 1946, but was back to nominal growth by 1947, and reached nearly 4 percent real growth by 1948.[42] Relative to widespread expectations of a return to depression, this recession was considered mild, and the expansion that followed was unprecedented.[43] Even in these relatively favorable economic conditions, President Truman found it difficult to muster public and congressional support for the Marshall Plan and containment efforts in Europe. The return of robust growth by 1946, however, made the job easier.

The years after the Vietnam War offered a mixed economic picture. The end of the war by itself did not trigger a sharp recession, as in the cases of the two world wars, but the mid-to-late 1970s were a time of oil embargoes, price shocks, and "stagflation." These economic concerns certainly were not the primary cause of Congress's increasing assertiveness on national security policy during the period, but they may have helped to strengthen Congress's hand.

The post-Cold War economy has mostly followed the pattern after World War I. The post-war contraction—in this case, the 1990-91 recession—was not particularly deep or long. But relative to high expectations of a "peace dividend," the austerity that

---

[41] Jim Potter, *The American Economy Between the World Wars* (Macmillan, 1985), p. 20.

[42] Arsen J. Darnay, ed., *Economic Indicators Handbook* (Gale Research Inc., 1992), p. 7.

[43] Andrew Graham with Anthony Sheldon, eds., *Government and Economies in the Postwar World* (Routledge, 1990), p. 231.

followed the Cold War seemed like an economic disappointment. The recovery that finally came was so weak as to lead to talk of a "double-dip" recession, with a trough that felt like six quarters rather than the actual three. This economic sluggishness, combined with other factors—the absence of any private sector job growth from 1989 to 1992, stagnant family median income from 1989 through 1993, large and widely-reported layoffs by major firms—fostered a widespread sense of economic insecurity even after robust economic growth returned. These economic concerns have "raised the bar" for new foreign policy initiatives in Congress, so that initiatives only tend to win support if they address specific security threats or can deliver tangible economic benefits at home.

Does the executive pursue bipartisan strategies with Congress? While the state of the world and the national economy may be the major determinants of executive-congressional relations on national security after a war, the executive branch's management of its dealings with Congress also matters. After World War I, President Wilson was high-handed with Congress. He did not include any members of Congress in the negotiation of the Treaty of Versailles or the League of Nations. He refused to accept modifications in the Treaty proposed by the Republican Senate and instead tried to go over Congress's head in a barnstorming trip meant to rally the public behind the new agreements. After World War II, in contrast, President Truman (himself a former Senator) and Secretary of State Dean Acheson—both acutely aware of Wilson's failure—worked closely with Senator Vandenberg and others. Describing an approach that might startle some modern-day executive branch officials, Acheson notes that he early recognized "the unwisdom of our trying to move any faster with a text than I could move in my discussions with Senators Connally and Vandenberg, since agreement would mean little unless it carried senatorial opinion with it."[44]

The post-Vietnam period saw both patterns. The White House reached out to members of Congress to advise or even participate on arms control negotiations. The Reagan administration attempt-

---

[44] Acheson, *op. cit.*, p. 277.

ed to increase bipartisan support for its policies in Central America through the Kissinger Commission. Yet the 1980s were mostly a time of partisan rancor on national security, with the Reagan and Bush administrations often pursuing policies on defense spending, arms control, aid to anti-communist movements, and human rights that galvanized Democrats into opposition.

The two administrations since the end of the Cold War have had a mixed record on bipartisanship. As the two case studies in the following chapters suggest, both administrations worked actively to create bipartisan support for some post-Cold War challenges, such as U.S. aid to former Soviet states, but hardly at all on others, such as peacekeeping.

Getting Down to Cases

At present, the four factors described above point in different directions, suggesting a mixed picture for post-Cold War executive-congressional relations—and since the end of the Cold War that is exactly what we have seen. But the mix is not random. Congress has been more or less assertive on *certain kinds* of national security issues and as a result of *certain kinds* of actions by the executive.

Not surprisingly, each issue is a microcosm for the broader trends in executive-congressional dynamics. The same factors that shaped the relationship after each war in the century are now determining outcomes on individual issues. That is, the post-Cold War executive branch is more likely to get its way the more any particular issue involves high security stakes, the more it can be framed as a continuation of the last war (that is, the Cold War), the more economic benefits are involved, and the more the president reaches out to both parties in Congress.

The next two chapters recount events on two issues that represent both sides of the current mix. The first case, the 1993 effort to increase aid to Russia and the other NIS, suggests that the executive is regaining some of its pre-Vietnam dominance. The administration proposed a sixfold increase in aid to these states and despite deep potential problems—tight budgets, partisan tensions, public opposition, turmoil in Russia—Congress completely fulfilled the President's request. In the second case, on multilateral peacekeeping in 1993 and 1994, Congress killed many of the administration's proposals, began driving many aspects of policy and funding, and turned the issue into a partisan and ideological flashpoint. In the first case, Congress agreed to let defense funds be used for non-defense purposes; in the second, it flatly refused. It is important to understand what accounted for the different outcomes.

2 Assistance to Russia and the Other Newly Independent States

The dissolution of the Soviet Union in late 1991 reshaped the global security environment and raised the question of what policies the U.S. should pursue toward its successor states. As a result, the issue of aid to Russia and the other newly independent states (NIS) of the former Soviet Union figured large in the 1992 presidential campaign. One of candidate Bill Clinton's most prominent foreign policy pledges was his call to increase U.S. assistance levels.[1] "Passing such aid," Clinton noted, "will require an act of political will by Congress and the President."[2]

In his first budget plan, released in April 1993, President Clinton proposed increasing assistance to Russia and the other NIS to $704 million, up from the $417 million proposed by the Bush administration in 1992.[3] Just two weeks later, following a summit with Russian President Boris Yeltsin, Clinton proposed to increase the Bush administration's figure by sixfold, up to $2.5 billion.

The political reaction was skeptical. The *Los Angeles Times*, citing the views of congressional Democrats, called the new bud-

---

[1] This commitment was stressed in all four of the major foreign policy speeches Clinton made during the campaign: "A New Covenant for American Security," Georgetown University, Washington, DC, December 12, 1991; Foreign Policy Association, New York, April 1, 1992; Los Angeles World Affairs Council, August 13, 1992; and Pabst Theater, Milwaukee, October 1, 1992.

[2] "Remarks Prepared for Delivery, Governor Bill Clinton," Foreign Policy Association, New York, April 1, 1992.

[3] *Budget of the United States : Fiscal Year 1994* (April, 1993), pp. A241-242. The federal fiscal year begins October 1; FY1994 runs from October 1993 through September 1994.

get target "difficult—perhaps impossible."[4] Sen. Patrick Leahy (D-VT), Chairman of the relevant Appropriations subcommittee, stated bluntly: "assuming that we do not hit the mega-bucks lotto, we have ourselves a problem. The money is not there."[5] A senior administration official who helped design the aid package said he harbored little hope at the time of obtaining the full amount from Congress: "It was an opening offer. I didn't think we'd get all the money."[6]

Just one week after the administration proposed the $2.5-billion package, the prospects for its passage dimmed further when the President's $16 billion domestic stimulus bill succumbed to a Republican filibuster in the Senate. In a heated hearing that day, Sen. Leahy told then-Ambassador-at-Large for Russia/NIS Strobe Talbott: "We have a jobs program. . . . on the floor for American jobs. That has been voted down. . . .   Now, we are going to be asked to vote . . . for a job program for Russians."[7] Nor was public opinion encouraging. Polls suggested that a solid majority of the American public opposed using more of their tax dollars to assist reform in Russia and its neighboring states.[8]

---

[4] "U.S. Pledges $1.8 Billion More in Aid to Russia," *Los Angeles Times* (April 15, 1993), p. A-12.

[5] Hearings: "Foreign Operations, Export Financing, and Related Programs Appropriations for Fiscal Year 1994," Senate Appropriations Committee, Subcommittee on Foreign Operations, Export Financing, and Related Programs (hereafter "Senate Foreign Operations Appropriations Hearings"), April 21, 1993.

[6] This and other unattributed quotations throughout this study are drawn from the author's interviews with senior administration officials, congressional staff, and members of Congress. As noted in the Introduction, interview subjects were told their names would be withheld in order to foster candor.

[7] Senate Foreign Operations Appropriations Hearings, *op cit.*

[8] A Gallup poll conducted in late March 1993 asked "Do you think the United States should increase financial aid to Russia, keep it the same as it is now, or decrease aid?" The poll found that 18 percent favored increasing aid, 46 percent favored keeping it at the same level, and 35 percent favored decreasing aid. Another Gallup poll conducted in late June 1993, asked: "Would you favor or oppose the United States increasing economic aid to Russia? Thirty-four percent favored the idea, while 64 percent opposed it. Polls taken during the 1992 presidential campaign found that voters would be less rather than more likely to support a candidate (50-29 percent) who favored "increasing U.S. economic aid to the former Soviet Republics (January 1992). Interestingly, voters perceived George Bush as favoring such an idea (77-11 percent), but incorrectly perceived Bill Clinton as *opposing* (32-28 percent) such an idea (Princeton Survey Research

Despite these early troubles, Congress worked through the spring and summer to craft a bill that ultimately provided $2,512,820,000—the president's full request, and then some—in assistance for Russia and the other NIS. The complex financing arrangement, however, required that the bill be enacted by midnight on September 30—the end of the fiscal year—after which $1.6 billion of the total would no longer be usable. On September 30, Congress gave the legislation its final approval. As evening fell, the bill was rushed across the city to the White House, and up to the president, who was at work in the Oval Office. At 7:15, with less than five hours to spare, President Clinton signed the package into law.

This chapter examines why—in the face of tight budgets, domestic needs, partisan tensions, lack of public support, and unsettling events in Russia—the administration and Congress were able to reach agreement on this initiative. It provides a case that seems to suggest an assertive executive and an almost deferential Congress after the end of the Cold War.

The Origins of the Assistance Package

Like all bills that become law, many factors contributed to the passage of the 1993 assistance package: related efforts in previous years, the way in which the administration developed its proposal, and dynamics within Congress. Each requires some examination.

American efforts to provide direct support for reform in the Soviet bloc began in earnest in 1989, as cracks began to show in Moscow's control over its empire. President Bush proposed an assistance package on April 17, immediately following the signing of the Polish "Roundtable Accord." On June 6, Rep. Lee

---

Associates/Times Mirror, May 1992); all polling from The Roper Center for Public Opinion Research. Some polls were somewhat more encouraging. An April 1993 New York Times/CBS poll reported that "52 percent of those polled said they were willing to support aid to Russia if it means averting civil war there, but that support fell to 41 percent when the economic aid was intended to 'help Russia reform its economy.' And only 29 percent favor offering such support if its aim is to keep Mr. Yeltsin . . . in power." Gwen Ifill, "President Urges America to Back Help for Moscow," *The New York Times* (April 2, 1993), p. A1.

Hamilton (D-IN) introduced the Democracy in Eastern Europe Act of 1989, which proposed assistance to Poland and Hungary. In October, House Foreign Affairs Committee Chairman Dante Fascell (D-FL) introduced the Support for East European Democracy (SEED) Act of 1989, which proposed over $900 million in assistance over three years. The SEED Act, together with the accompanying funding, was passed by Congress and signed into law in late November.[9]

As the Soviet Union began to dissolve, Congress turned its attention to direct assistance for reform and demilitarization in the states that would succeed it. One of the most important efforts was an August 1991 proposal by then-Rep. Les Aspin (D-WI), chairman of the House Armed Services Committee, to use $1 billion of defense funds to provide humanitarian aid to the Soviet Union. That fall, Aspin joined with his Senate counterpart, Sen. Sam Nunn (D-GA), in attempting to add such a provision to the annual defense authorization bill. As noted in Chapter 1, their effort died for lack of support from the Bush administration and other members of Congress, but it was partially revived in a bill signed into law on December 12, 1991, which authorized the President to use up to $100 million in defense funds to support humanitarian assistance and up to $400 million for denuclearization (this portion became known as the "Nunn-Lugar" program).[10]

The first major package of bilateral aid for Russia came the next year, when the Bush administration won passage of the Freedom Support Act.[11] The Bush administration invested heavily in the bill's passage: Secretary of State James Baker lobbied for it personally; the administration brought Ambassador Robert Strauss back from Russia so he could contribute his congressional skills. The final legislation, signed October 24, authorized about $400 million for a range of activities, including humanitarian assistance, promotion of democratic reform, economic privatization, and environmental protection.

---

[9] The Democracy in Eastern Europe Act of 1989 was H.R. 2550. The SEED Act was H.R. 3402, enacted as PL 101-179.

[10] The bill was H.J. Res. 157, enacted as PL 102-229.

[11] The bill was S. 2532, enacted as PL 102-511.

These efforts, particularly the Freedom Support Act, helped lay the foundations for the passage of the 1993 package. Having been enacted by a Republican administration and Democratic Congress, they set precedents for bipartisan cooperation on these issues. Moreover, the Bush White House, Congress, and many advocacy groups had mounted extensive outreach efforts, including briefings on the Freedom Support Act for business leaders and ethnic-American groups. Both the bipartisan relationships and the outreach networks became assets in the Clinton administration's efforts to expand the levels of aid.[12]

The 1992 presidential campaign also helped set the stage for the 1993 package of assistance. One of candidate Clinton's main criticisms of President Bush's foreign policy record was that Bush was "overly cautious on the issue of aid to Russia."[13] Following similar criticisms by some Republicans, especially former President Nixon, the Bush administration accelerated development of its aid package (which became the Freedom Support Act).[14] It announced its initiative on April 1, 1992—the same day Governor Clinton delivered a major foreign policy address stressing the issue. This race to "own" the issue helped to elevate it and give it a bipartisan face.

The Clinton Administration Develops its Proposal

Within its first weeks in office, the Clinton administration's foreign policy team began crafting a Russia/NIS aid package. Starting on February 6, 1993, and continuing throughout the next three months, a senior team met to decide overall strategy toward Russia and the other NIS. That group typically included the President, Vice President Gore, Secretary of State Christopher, National Security Adviser Anthony Lake, his Deputy, Samuel "Sandy"

---

[12] For example, during consideration of the Freedom Support Act, Rep. David Nagle (D-IA) convened regular meetings of advocacy groups and ethnic-American organizations who could lobby in favor of the bill. Although Nagle lost his re-election bid in 1992, he helped reassemble the coalition to press for passage of the 1993 bill.

[13] Speech to the Foreign Policy Association, April 1, 1992.

[14] See Marvin Kalb, *The Nixon Memo* (University of Chicago Press, 1994).

Berger, Ambassador-at-Large Talbott, National Security Adviser to the Vice President Leon Fuerth, NSC staffers Toby Gati and Nicholas Burns, and presidential adviser George Stephanopoulos.

From the start, the effort to craft a strategy toward Russia and the other NIS had the benefit of the President's direct interest in the subject. One participant noted: "We never had 'senior adviser' meetings on this; they were all presidential meetings." One of the ways in which the President signalled his interest in the issue had been his selection of his close friend, Strobe Talbott, to be the "czar" for policy toward Russia and the NIS. The impact of that choice on the internal policy making process was substantial. "There was no foreign policy issue that could contend with us," a senior presidential aide noted. "Nobody would dare cross Strobe at that point."

The President and this advisory group decided, among other things, to label support for reform in Russia and the other NIS Clinton's "number one priority" in foreign policy. They decided to schedule an early summit (April 3) with President Yeltsin and to make that summit in Vancouver, British Columbia, President Clinton's first trip outside the United States. They also decided to develop a major package of assistance for Russia and the NIS and to seek additional support from other Group of Seven (G-7) nations and multilateral financial institutions. All this was intended to signal the importance the President placed on this issue—a signal aimed not only at Russia but also at Congress.

The President decided he would announce at the summit a $1.6-billion package of assistance. This package was composed of funds already appropriated—although not all of the funds had been slated to go to Russia. Yet even before he left for the summit, the President had decided to propose an additional package of assistance, composed of new funds.[15]

On March 18, the Russia team met with the President to suggest the shape of such a package. They proposed a total of $1 bil-

---

[15] The President suggested this in his remarks in Vancouver, when he said that he would go back and approach Congress about "broader cooperative initiatives" beyond the $1.6 billion package." The President's News Conference with President Boris Yeltsin in Vancouver, April 4, 1993," *Papers of the President: William J. Clinton, 1993, Book One* (Government Printing Office, 1994), p. 393.

lion, nearly 50 percent more than the $700 million already adopt-
ed by the administration for its FY1994 budget. The figure had
been developed, in part, on the basis of the judgments of Talbott
and career staff at State about what Congress would support.
According to participants, the President's reaction was, "Not bold
enough." He told the team: "You guys go out and be bold. Tell
me what you think substantively needs to be done. Don't worry
about how Congress will react to the price tag. I'll worry about
Congress. That's my job—to sell it to the Hill."

Not all administration officials agreed with the President's
instincts. Some senior political aides thought a bold foreign aid
bill would interfere with attempts to pass the President's budget
and other domestic initiatives. A different political problem was
added to the equation on March 20, when President Yeltsin
announced an April 25 national referendum and said he was prepared to take extra-constitutional measures in order to settle his
disputes with his parliament. President Clinton, however, issued
a statement within hours of Yeltsin's announcement, stressing
that "as Russia's only democratically elected national leader, he
has our support."[16]

Despite real and potential political worries, the President persisted in demanding a more ambitious package. At one point, at
an April 6 meeting, he even suggested that a popular program
toward Russia and the other NIS might help, rather than hurt, his
efforts to get Congress to fund domestic programs, such as the
stimulus package; Clinton told his aides: "I want some of those
guys out there committed to spending billions for Russia so they
have to explain why they won't spend anything on the U.S."

The Russia team and their staff developed several new
options, with one totaling $5 billion. Ultimately, the highest
option presented to the President was $2.5 billion, and at the
meeting on April 6, this figure was adopted. The administration's
package contained a mix of housing for military officers returning from the Baltic countries; privatization assistance; assistance
to Russia's agricultural, energy, and environmental sectors;
exchanges; humanitarian assistance; and other efforts.

---

[16] Statement of the President, March 20, 1993.

The administration intended not to unveil the details of the package and the total price tag until later in the spring or even in the summer. As a result, the individual elements of the package were never reviewed with members of Congress, nor did the package include any proposal for how to finance the increase in assistance. But many elements reflected congressional preferences that had been heard in earlier consultations and during the effort to pass the Freedom Support Act. For example, administration officials understood the political appeal of programs that could promote U.S. exports and agricultural sales. One member of the advisory team noted: "We knew certain things were politically easier to get, like wheat, because of interest from people like Dole, even when such elements may not have been the best thing to do."

The package also anticipated congressional political sensitivities. For example, during the February 6 meeting of the Russia team at the State Department, Ambassador Talbott stressed the need to address Russia's tattered "social safety net." State Department Counselor (and later Undersecretary) Timothy Wirth, who had just retired from the Senate, injected some legislative wisdom: "Strobe, if you call it that, Congress will eat you alive, because we've got a social safety net crisis here in the U.S." From then on, funds to address the social consequences of Russia's transitions consistently were labeled "privatization."

In mid-April, a week after the President had settled on the $2.5-billion target, Secretary Christopher and Treasury Secretary Lloyd Bentsen flew to Tokyo for a G-7 summit. The meeting had been convened by President Clinton to develop multilateral responses to the challenge of reform in Russia and the other NIS. At the summit, Secretary Bentsen mistakenly divulged the proposed $2.5-billion figure to the press, and the administration's new goal became public.

The Administration Takes its Proposal to Congress

The job of persuading Congress to provide such a sizable sum began even before the Vancouver summit. On March 25 and 26, the President hosted two dinners at the White House for the congressional leaders of both parties and the chairmen and ranking Republicans of each of the committees with a stake in decisions on Russia and the NIS. The first was for representatives, the second for senators. The two dinners were among the first major meetings between the President and Congress on national security policy.

According to those present, the President made a compelling and even a "passionate" case. He argued that the course of reform in Russia and the other republics was crucial to U.S. national security interests. He stressed that he planned to use U.S. aid to leverage additional assistance from other nations. He noted it would be a hard year to appropriate funds for this purpose and stated that it must be a bipartisan effort to be successful. He then went around the room to hear comments and suggestions from the members. Many of them stressed particular program areas, such as food aid, assistance to Russia's energy sector, space cooperation, housing for military officers returning from the Baltics, and exchanges for students and business people.

The response from many members was strong. According to one participant at the dinner for House members, "the Democratic members were supportive, but the Republican members were maybe even *more* supportive. In particular, Newt [Gingrich] answered a great speech from the President with a great speech of his own. He said that this was one of the great, defining moments of our time; that it could not be a partisan issue; and that if the President were willing to commit to this personally and make the case to the public, Republicans in Congress would stand by him."

The response at the dinner for senators was equally supportive and bipartisan. Sen. Lugar said that "the President's statements are historic and right." Sen. Warner said that he "commend[ed] the President's support" for assistance to Russia and the other Soviet successor states. Like Rep. Gingrich, Sen. Leahy stressed that the president needed to make the case to the public.

The President began making the public case on April 1, just before leaving for the Vancouver summit. In a speech to newspaper editors delivered at the Annapolis Naval Academy, Clinton called for "a strategic alliance with Russian reform." He stressed that the highest security interests were at stake: "The danger is clear if Russia's reforms turn sour—if it reverts to authoritarianism or disintegrates into chaos. The world cannot afford the strife of the former Yugoslavia replicated in a nation as big as Russia, spanning eleven time zones with an armed arsenal of nuclear weapons. . . ." He also stressed the domestic benefits of a peaceful, democratic Russia, such as lower defense spending and increased trade: "Our ability to put people first at home requires that we put Russia and its neighbors first on our agenda abroad."[17]

The speech was intended to signal the President's commitment and to build domestic support for the assistance effort. A senior official who has worked for both Democratic and Republican administrations noted: "it's a Washington thing. It's one thing for a president to stand up at a congressional dinner to say that he wants something. It's another thing to say it in a prepared text before the nation. We didn't think the Annapolis speech would reach everyone in Dubuque. It was aimed at Congress and the Russians. In Washington, speeches are important." Comments by a congressional committee staff director suggest the signal was received: "The dinners and speeches sent a message that this is something the White House and the President care about."

The Gephardt-Michel Delegation

Congress's efforts on the SEED Act, the Nunn-Lugar provisions, and the Freedom Support Act created a base of congressional expertise and bipartisan familiarity with many elements of the FY1994 package. Yet all those initiatives had been enacted under a Republican administration. Even with their own party's president leading the charge, in October 1992, House Republicans had split nearly evenly on the final Freedom Support Act vote (78-77 favoring the conference report). It was not clear whether Republican members of Congress would continue to support such initiatives under a Democratic administration.

One of the keys to retaining that support, and to the bill's final passage, was a congressional delegation that traveled to Russia and Ukraine in April 1993. The trip was conceived by Majority Leader Richard Gephardt (D-MO) and co-chaired by

---

[17] Ifill, *op. cit.*, p. A1.

Minority Leader Robert Michel (R-IL). The bipartisan delegation they assembled read like a Who's Who of the House leadership and members needed to pass the bill. According to one seasoned Hill staffer: "It was as high profile of a substantive delegation as I've ever seen in my 15 years here."

Rep. Gephardt's decision to organize the delegation reflected two factors. The first was the high priority he placed on support for Russian reform. According to a former aide, "Dick decided long ago that Russia was the number one most important national security issue, principally due to their nukes."[18] The second was his judgment that "it was necessary to build a bipartisan foundation for this that would endure."

The Gephardt-Michel delegation was a turning point for Congress. According to one aide who went on the trip: "Members were impressed with the magnitude of what had to be accomplished there. They saw young, friendly faces of the new Russian leadership juxtaposed with old Soviet men who were never going to change."

The most frequently mentioned event on the trip was the delegation's meeting with Russian Vice President Alexandr Rutskoi, in his spacious office, filled with models of military hardware and large wall maps. One of the maps was of the pre-1991 Soviet Union. One of the congressmen asked: "Isn't that map a bit out of date?" Rutskoi responded: "Maybe now; maybe not in the future." According to one congressman on the trip, "it was a frightening reality check."

The delegation returned committed to support dramatic action. Their trip report to the President—which was signed by every member in the delegation—concluded:

> The delegation believes that the United States and its allies should show a strong sense of urgency in addressing and assisting the transformation. . . . American opinion and leadership is very important to the Russian people. If the United

---

[18] Gephardt had signalled his commitment to the issue in a March 6, 1990 speech, in which he sounded the first major congressional call for direct assistance to the Soviet Union. The speech provoked sharp criticism, not only from the Bush administration, but also from a broad and bipartisan range of members of Congress and pundits.

States clearly expresses confidence in the Russian reform process and in President Yeltsin, as its current leader, our influence can be felt. . . . The United States cannot afford <u>not</u> to help the Russian people. . . . Our national interest is deeply and lastingly affected by what happens in the former Soviet Union.[19]

Congress Acts: The House

Despite the base of support created by the Gephardt-Michel delegation and the assistance packages from previous years, the 1993 bill got off to a troubled start. As noted earlier, there was initial skepticism that Congress could find $2.5 billion. A key House staffer says: "We couldn't believe the number at first. The White House got out ahead of itself with a number it had no way of achieving."

Probably more unsettling to the key members of Congress, the unveiling of the $2.5-billion figure in Tokyo on April 14 caught them completely by surprise. There are few things more infuriating to a member of Congress than being blindsided by an administration proposal—particularly if the member chairs a committee of jurisdiction. Yet Sen. Leahy's office first heard about the $2.5-billion proposal when a reporter phoned in from Japan to get the chairman's reaction.[20] Leahy's counterpart in the House, Rep. David Obey (D-WI), had a similar reaction; according to one staffer: "He was P.O.'d. He was upset about the dollar level and upset about not being talked to."

The congressional environment became even more hostile over the next week as the President's $16-billion domestic stimulus package was defeated by a Senate filibuster. Sen. Robert Byrd

---

[19] "CODEL [congressional delegation] Gephardt-Michel: Trip Report" (April 1993).

[20] Leahy had been angry at the Bush administration over its proposal to write off $7 billion in Egyptian debt because he first learned of the effort by reading about it in the *Washington Post*. He had warned President Clinton early in the new administration: "Don't surprise me." According to several sources, Leahy was furious to be caught unaware by a president of his own Party. According to one source: "This was a seminal event. He went ahead, but it was with anger and bitterness throughout."

(D-WV) accused Republicans of "murdering" this centerpiece of the President's economic agenda, while Sen. Orrin Hatch (R-UT) noted that the filibuster had created a more divided, partisan atmosphere: "Bill Clinton has succeeded in doing something George Bush never did; he united the Senate Republicans."[21] Yet despite these missteps and obstacles, there emerged a clear determination among key members in both parties to make good on the President's commitment.

One of the most important signs of that determination was the intensive effort by Rep. Obey to assemble the financing for the assistance package. Obey had a long-standing interest in the issue—his Master's degree had been in Soviet studies—and, along with others such as Rep. Gephardt, he had been one of the early advocates of direct assistance to Russia. Now, despite being caught by surprise by the administration's proposal, he became the architect for the means to finance it. According to those who participated, Rep. Obey and his staff began "by squeezing absolutely everything else" in the international affairs account.[22] Next, they saw that there was unused budget authority remaining in the current fiscal year, FY1993—about $600 million for the Foreign Operations subcommittee and about $1 billion for the Defense subcommittee.

It was easy enough for Rep. Obey to tap the unused budget authority from his own subcommittee for the new bill, but efforts to use defense money for foreign aid generally, and especially for Russia/NIS aid, were problematic. In particular, House Defense subcommittee chair, Rep. John Murtha (D-PA), had been resistant to the idea of using defense funds in Russia and the other NIS for anything other than demilitarization—and even then he had reservations.

---

[21] Adam Clymer, "G.O.P. Senators Prevail, Sinking Clinton's Economic Stimulus Bill, *The New York Times* (April 22, 1993), p. A1.

[22] Under the final legislation, many major accounts sustained deep cuts in order to make room for the assistance to Russia and the other NIS. Funding for multilateral financial institutions was cut about $500 million from the administration's request. The bill funded development assistance at a level more than $100 million under the administration's request. The Economic Support Fund was funded at about $300 million less than the preceding year. The administration's request for anti-narcotics activities, about $150 million, was cut by about one-third.

Obey's staff approached Murtha's staff to discuss the Defense subcommittee's unused budget authority. According to one participant, "their first reaction was, 'Hell no.' Murtha has not been enthusiastic about [Nunn-Lugar]. He's been more interested in protecting military pay and readiness at a time of military downsizing. Of course, the staff reaction on Defense is 'hell no' because everyone wants to raid their funds. Murtha had to protect his flank. If someone saw us tapping his money for Russia, then people would start asking what else you could use it for."

The only chance to obtain the needed defense funds for the package was a direct appeal by Chairman Obey to Chairman Murtha. The two met in the conference room of the full Appropriations committee. Obey said, "Look, this is the end of the Cold War. You've got to do this." Murtha was more receptive than expected.

Rep. Murtha's willingness to cooperate stemmed in part from the administration's steady attention to him. Both Howard Paster, Chief of White House legislative affairs, and Leon Panetta, at that time Director of the Office of Management and Budget (OMB), had lobbied him on the Russian aid package. In addition, the President had worked on building a bridge to the powerful chairman during private meetings and golf outings. An administration official described the first private session between the two this way: "It was a no-agenda meeting. Purely social. The two of them sat down together on the yellow wing-back chairs in the Oval Office. After a little while, the President calls in the steward for some coffee. When the steward comes in, he turns to Murtha and asks, 'are you hungry?' Murtha says, 'yeah.' So the President asks the steward to bring them a couple of big pieces of pie. Well, after you've got him there in the Oval Office, in those yellow chairs, with both of them sitting with a piece of pie balanced on their knees, then you've got a friend."

Once Reps. Obey and Murtha had worked out a basic agreement and discussed it with members of the leadership and other key members, formal action in the House proceeded quickly. On May 26, Rep. Obey's Foreign Operations Appropriations Subcommittee approved a bill by voice vote that included the $2.5 billion for Russia/NIS. The full House Appropriations Committee took up the bill on June 10. Rep. Sonny Callahan (R-AL) attempted to strip the funds for Russia and the other NIS. He cited, in particular, the support for housing for Russian troops returning from the Baltics: "We're downsizing 3,000 military people a week in this country and we're not giving them any housing." But the bipartisan support assembled earlier prevailed. Rep. Robert Livingston (R-LA), who had been part of the Gephardt-Michel delegation, countered: "We are talking about the single most important move this country could make for future generations."[23] Callahan's motion was defeated, and the bill was adopted by the full Committee on a voice vote.

The package was brought to the House floor a week later, on June 17. Prospects for passage generally looked good. Just the day before, the House had managed to pass the Foreign Aid Authorization bill—legislation that had not made it into law since 1985—and had fended off an amendment to delete authorization for much of the funding for Russia and the other NIS.[24] Even so, there were rumors the Congressional Black Caucus (CBC) would oppose the assistance provisions, just as many of its members the previous year had opposed the Freedom Support Act. As a result, the administration worked the vote hard. Defense Secretary Aspin sent a letter to members indicating his support for the use of defense funds in the bill. The President sent a letter to all members urging passage and stressing the administration's bipartisan efforts in developing its aid proposal.[25]

As it turned out, there was some opposition from CBC members. CBC chairman, Rep. Kweisi Mfume (D-MD) spoke in favor when Rep. Callahan offered an amendment to strike the $1.6 billion in supplemental funds from the bill:[26] "To defeat the domestic stimulus package in April and then somehow mysteriously

---

[23] "$2.5 Billion Approved for Ex-Soviet States," *Congressional Quarterly Almanac, 1993*, p. 606.

[24] The amendment was defeated by a vote of 118-317. As it turned out, in 1993, the Foreign Aid authorization bill once again failed to reach enactment; it never made it to the floor of the Senate.

[25] Letter from President Clinton to Speaker of the House Tom Foley, June 16, 1993.

[26] That is, the approximately $1 billion in FY1993 Defense budget authority, and about $600 million in FY1993 Foreign Operations budget authority.

pass Russian aid in June would create the perception that our priorities are in the wrong place."[27] About half the Black Caucus (17 of 38) agreed. So did a majority of House Republicans (93-79). House freshmen voted to cut the funds for Russia and the other NIS by about 7 percentage points more than non-freshmen, a gap that was reflected in both parties. But the division among the Republicans combined with an overwhelming Democratic vote (46-210 against the amendment), was enough to save the funds for Russia and the other NIS. Callahan's amendment lost by a wide margin, 140-289. Ultimately, the entire bill passed the House easily, 309-111, with a solid majority of Republicans—107 to 63— joining most Democrats in voting for passage.

Congress Acts: The Senate

The administration and some in Congress were eager to gain quick Senate approval as well. But tensions between Congress and the administration on national security were beginning to rise—principally over the U.S. mission in Somalia. And there were problems with the Foreign Operations bill.

First, Sen. Daniel Inouye (D-HI), Chairman of the Senate Defense Appropriations Subcommittee, was not yet prepared to follow Rep. Murtha's lead in allowing nearly $1 billion of defense money to be used for Russia and the other NIS. While Sen. Inouye was generally sympathetic to foreign aid—he had previously chaired the Foreign Operations subcommittee—he was concerned about the impact of this expenditure on the Defense Department budget for the coming year.[28]

Second, there was an arcane problem involving loan guarantees for Israel. Under federal budgeting rules, Congress had to appropriate a fraction of the value of the guarantees as a hedge

---

[27] *Congressional Quarterly Almanac, 1993, op. cit.*, p. 607.

[28] Congress focuses most on two measures of each account in the federal budget: budget authority and outlays. The first is the up-front grant of authority to spend funds. Outlays are actual expenditures. A bill that approves $1 in budget authority in a given year often results in several years of outlays that add up to this sum. The $1 billion in defense funds in this bill was budget authority; it was estimated at the time that these funds would be spent over several years, with approximately $210 million to be spent during the first year, FY1994.

against possible default on the loans. But setting these funds aside would make it virtually impossible to fund the entire $2.5 billion.

As the end of the fiscal year drew near, concerns mounted that the full $2.5 billion simply could not be obtained. As in the House, the impasse could only be broken by a direct meeting of the principals. In early September, Sen. Inouye and Sen. Leahy met with two other key players—Senate Appropriations Chairman Byrd and Budget Committee Chairman Jim Sasser (D-TN). According to participants, the meeting was "difficult" and at times "acrimonious." Sen. Leahy laid out the general case for the Russian aid package. Sen. Byrd then spoke firmly in favor of the effort, stressing the need to support "a young president who is willing to make some hard decisions here and take some political risks." Sen. Byrd apparently gained Sen. Inouye's cooperation simply by asking him for it—direct requests from an Appropriations Committee chairman are hard to refuse—and by stressing his own willingness, as part of the solution, to support the Israeli loan guarantee provision. This was an important consideration for Sen. Inouye, who is one of the most ardent congressional supporters of aid to Israel, and a major concession from Sen. Byrd, who is not.

Finding a way to eliminate the accounting cost of the Israeli loan guarantees was more difficult. Some of those present proposed that Sen. Sasser exercise his prerogative as Budget Committee chairman and direct the Congressional Budget Office (CBO), in essence, to assume the Israeli loans bore no default risk. Sen. Sasser refused to do so, arguing that directing the CBO in this way would weaken the integrity of the congressional budget process. He suggested an alternative: that, in essence, the Senate agree not to count this expense against the overall budget caps set in the 1990 budget deal worked out between Congress and President Bush. But as one of the negotiators in 1990, Sen. Byrd held a passionate commitment to these caps. He also objected to this approach because it would make the entire bill vulnerable to a budgetary point of order on the Senate floor, which would require 60 votes to overcome. Finally, however, Sen. Byrd agreed to exempt the provision from the 1990 budget caps.

Why did the powerful Appropriations chairman embrace such an exceptional package? Part of the answer lay in historical circumstance. The meeting occurred just as Israel and PLO were forging their breakthrough declaration. According to one participant in the meeting: "people were saying, 'my God! Can you believe Rabin and Arafat are shaking hands?' And, second, they believed Russia was too important to mess up." Another factor in the support of Sen. Byrd—and many other members—was former President Nixon. Some weeks earlier, Sen. Byrd and about a dozen Senate colleagues of both parties had met with the former president to hear his reasons for supporting aid to Russia and the other NIS. The meeting reportedly had a significant impact on Sen. Byrd and the others present. Like the Gephardt-Michel delegation, it appears to have been a major factor in firming up bipartisan support for the initiative.

Once these four senators reached agreement, things moved quickly. Sen. Leahy's Appropriations Subcommittee met September 13—only hours after the Israeli-PLO handshake—and approved the bill by voice vote. The full Appropriations committee approved the bill unanimously the next day.

History intervened a week later, on September 21, when President Yeltsin disbanded Russia's Parliament and called for December elections. President Clinton quickly signaled his support for Yeltsin, calling him the same day and issuing a White House press statement that said, "As the democratically-elected leader of Russia, President Yeltsin has chosen to allow the people of Russia themselves to resolve this impasse . . . and I support him fully."

There was broad concern about the impact that the tumultuous events in Russia would have on the aid package in Congress. Sen. Leahy said it would be "a real roll of the dice" to bring the bill to the floor. Yet when the legislation was taken up by the Senate the next day, September 22, many Senators cited the events in Russia as a reason to vote for—not against—the bill. Sen. Mitch McConnell, the ranking Republican on Sen. Leahy's subcommittee, said that "the events in the past few days [make] our support for democracy and economic reform . . . more important than ever."[29] *Congressional Quarterly* noted that, "senators followed Clinton's lead in rallying around the Russian presi-

---

[29] *Congressional Record* (September 22, 1993), p. S 12221.

dent."[30] The bill passed the next day, 88-10, with Republicans voting 36-7 in favor.

The budget point of order that had worried Sen. Byrd was never raised on the Senate floor. In part, this was because Senators Byrd, Leahy, Inouye, and Sasser, soon after their meeting, consulted with several key Republicans and obtained their support. At that point, other potential opponents abandoned any thought of blocking or cutting the aid package. Sen. Helms, for example—then the ranking Republican on the Senate Foreign Relations Committee—was one of the strongest critics of the administration, of foreign aid, and of using defense funds for non-defense purposes, as this bill did. Yet, one of Sen. Helms's aides says this: "We knew about the budget point of order. But Nunn, [ranking Republican on the Armed Services Committee, Sen. Strom] Thurmond and Lugar were comfortable with the impact on defense; [ranking Republican on the Budget Committee, Sen. Pete] Domenici was supportive; and Dole thought it was imperative to pass the package."

The House and Senate quickly moved to conference committee, so that the final bill could be crafted before both the fiscal year and the financing package expired. The conferees quickly negotiated compromises on the over 100 differences between the two chambers' versions of the bill. Few of the changes affected the provisions on Russia and the other NIS, although the conferees agreed to eliminate Senate "earmarks" for Ukraine and Armenia; instead they simply urged the administration to allocate $300 million and $18 million, respectively, to these two nations.

The House approved the conference report on September 29, 321-108. The Senate followed suit the next day, 88-11. Congressional aides hurriedly prepared the final bill and rushed it across town to the White House, where it was carried directly into the Oval Office for President Clinton's signature.

Epilogue

The 1993 bill looks like a case of a strong executive branch and a relatively docile Congress after the Cold War. Congress funded

---

[30] *Congressional Quarterly Almanac, 1993, op. cit.*, p. 609.

the President's entire aid proposal despite tight budgets, administration missteps, and chaotic events in Russia. With broad bipartisanship, Congress bent budget rules, provided the funds with virtually no earmarks, permitted the defense budget to be used for non-defense purposes, and expedited passage of the legislation.

One can argue that the early months of 1993 were an atypical period, particularly on this issue—that the Clinton presidency and the Yeltsin government were both enjoying honeymoons in Congress. To be sure, a series of events since the fall of 1993 has tarnished U.S.-Russian relations and soured Congress's attitude toward Russian aid: the election of ultra-nationalist Vladimir Zhironovsky and a large block of anti-reform members of Parliament in the December 1993 elections; President Yeltsin's dismissal of several reform-minded ministers; the arrest of CIA double agent Aldrich Ames in February 1994; Russian efforts to exert influence in the "near abroad"; Russia's affinity with the Serbs in the Bosnian peace process; its proposed sale of nuclear reactors to Iran; and the brutality of Russia's efforts to suppress Chechnya's bid for independence. Such events have led several Republican members to criticize the Clinton administration for an excessively "Russia first" orientation in its policy toward the region.

Yet the honeymoon between Clinton and Congress on national security had largely ended by September 1993, as the next chapter makes clear. And despite the souring of U.S.-Russian relations, Congress has not blocked much of the Clinton's administration's program toward Russia in the months that have followed. In 1994, for example, the administration proposed that assistance to Russia and the other NIS should total $900 million; Congress appropriated $850 million. As this study goes to press, the House is voting on legislation that would restrict some aid to Russia if Moscow sold nuclear reactors to Iran or failed to moderate its behavior toward Chechnya, but President Clinton has threatened to veto the bill, and its future remains in question. Chapter 4 suggests some reasons why Congress has continued giving the administration most of what it has proposed on this issue, and why it may well continue to do so.

3 Peacekeeping

One of the central post-Cold War stories in the relationship between the executive branch and Congress has been their mutual effort to shape new U.S. policies for peacekeeping.[1] Unlike the 1993 Russia/NIS aid bill, however, the work of the two branches on peacekeeping during 1993-94 increasingly was driven by Congress.

With the superpower stand-off gone, many observers reasoned it would be easier for the United Nations and other multilateral bodies to police security threats and enforce peace agreements. The prominent role of the United Nations in sanctioning the Gulf War bolstered the view that the organization could finally fulfill this part of its founding vision. The initial optimism toward peace-keeping was broadly held. UN peacekeepers won the 1988 Nobel Peace Prize. In 1992, UN Secretary General Boutros-Ghali issued a report promoting preventive diplomacy and peace operations as well as calling for the creation of standing UN forces.[2] President Bush told the UN General Assembly in 1992 with regard to peace-keeping, "as much as the United Nations has done, it can do much more."[3] In December 1992, he deployed over 27,000 U.S. troops to

---

[1] The term peacekeeping is used here to encompass the full range of multi-lateral peace operations, including both non-combat operations conducted with the consent of both parties within the context of a viable peace accord and "hot" military operations conducted without consent or without a viable cease-fire or peace agreement in effect.

[2] Boutros Boutros-Ghali, *An Agenda for Peace: Preventive Diplomacy, Peacemaking and Peace-keeping*, Report of the Secretary General (United Nations, January 1992).

[3] Address to the UN General Assembly, September 21, 1992, in *Public Papers of the Presidents of the United States: George Bush*, p. 1599.

help relieve famine in Somalia. That same month, former President Reagan said that "we should rely more on multilateral institutions" and called for a standing UN "army of conscience."[4]

As hopes for peacekeeping expanded, so did the number of UN operations. In the 40 years from 1948 to 1987, the United Nations had deployed thirteen peacekeeping missions. In the five years from 1988 through 1992, it deployed fourteen.[5]

Candidate Bill Clinton echoed the new optimism about peace-keeping in his campaign for the presidency, declaring that "multilateral action holds promise as never before." He pledged to explore new initiatives such as a UN rapid deployment force and to have the United States pay its UN bills for peacekeeping and other activities in full.[6]

Over the next two years, however, peacekeeping became the single most contentious and partisan national security issue between the administration and Congress.[7] Congress killed two major administration initiatives to fund some peacekeeping costs out of the defense budget and confronted the executive branch with proposals to: cut off funds for U.S. forces in Somalia and Rwanda; restrict the deployment of U.S. troops to Haiti; bar the service of U.S. forces in peacekeeping under foreign commanders; prohibit the use of defense funds for paying peacekeeping assess-

---

[4] "Democracy's Next Battle," Address to the Oxford Union Society, Oxford, England, December 4, 1992.

[5] Testimony of Frank C. Conahan, Assistant Comptroller General, General Accounting Office, "U.N. Peacekeeping: Observations on Mandates and Operational Capability," Subcommittee on Terrorism, Narcotics, and International Operations, Committee on Foreign Relations, U.S. Senate, June 9, 1993.

[6] Address to the Foreign Policy Association, New York, April 1, 1992; address to the Los Angeles World Affairs Council, August 13, 1992.

[7] Two sets of numbers reveal the contentiousness between the two branches over peacekeeping. First, votes on peacekeeping—including Somalia, Haiti, and Bosnia—accounted for 60 percent (6 out of 10) of the contested votes on which the Clinton administration's position did not prevail in the 103rd Congress (1993-94). Second, of the 17 contested peacekeeping votes on which the administration's position did prevail, 82 percent (14 of 17) would have had a different outcome if only Republicans had been voting; in contrast, of the 39 non-peacekeeping con-tested votes on which the administration's position prevailed, only 18 percent (7 of 39) would have had a different outcome if only Republicans had been voting.

ments; withhold a portion of U.S. peacekeeping assessments unless certain UN reforms were implemented; require reports to Congress on new or changed UN peacekeeping mandates; and increase the pressure for UN reimbursement of all Pentagon expenses in support of UN operations.

Restrictions on peacekeeping became a plank of the "Contract With America," the Republicans' manifesto for their landslide congressional victory, and most of these provisions were adopted in the House, largely along party lines. Similar restrictions on peacekeeping were also the centerpiece of one of the first bills introduced by new Senate Majority Leader Dole.[8]

Why did peacekeeping change from a field of broad agreement to an arena for congressional assertiveness? A major part of the answer clearly lies in the failures of peacekeeping on the ground—the death of 18 American servicemen in Somalia on October 3, 1993; the inability of UN peacekeepers to stem the war in the former Yugoslavia; the failed attempt by the *USS Harlan County* to land military trainers in Haiti in mid-October 1993—and the controversial deployment of U.S. troops to Haiti in the fall of 1994.

The events in Somalia, Bosnia, and Haiti are not sufficient to explain Congress's recent actions on peacekeeping, however. After all, public opinion on peacekeeping generally remained favorable—even *after* the American deaths in Somalia. A February 1994 poll found that 84 percent of Americans favored the idea of UN peacekeeping operations; numerous post-Somalia polls found that a majority of Americans still felt the United States should contribute troops to such operations.[9] Moreover, congressional antipathy toward peacekeeping was *selective*. While Congress voted to restrict peacekeeping in many ways, it also voted in mid-1994 to approve $1.2 billion to pay past and future peacekeeping bills—the largest peacekeeping appropriation ever.

One might also explain the emergence of peacekeeping as a divisive issue by pointing to partisan motives. Clearly, there is merit to this answer: congressional Republicans used attacks on

---

[8] "The Peace Powers Act of 1995," S. 5, introduced on January 5.

[9] Steven Kull and Clay Ramsay, *U.S. Public Attitudes on UN Peacekeeping* (Program on International Policy Attitudes, March, 1994), pp. 5-7.

peacekeeping to support a larger critique of President Clinton's stewardship of U.S. national security. Yet this point is circular. The real question is why Congress turned peacekeeping into a partisan issue when it did not do so on other issues, such as the 1993 Russia/NIS aid package.

Unlike the case of aid to Russia and the other NIS, the story of executive-congressional relations on peacekeeping cannot be retold in the context of a single bill. Instead, during 1993-94, the executive branch and Congress confronted a series of interrelated questions regarding general peacekeeping policy, the conduct of specific peacekeeping missions, and funding for UN peacekeeping bills. Although action on all three of these fronts proceeded simultaneously, this chapter looks first at peacekeeping policy and missions, and then in some depth at peacekeeping funding. The picture that emerges is that of an assertive Congress that drove peacekeeping policy and rejected repeated executive proposals for peacekeeping funding.

Peacekeeping Policy and Missions

President Clinton's peacekeeping policy narrowed steadily during his administration's first two years, as optimistic theory collided with grim events on the ground and strong challenges in Congress. Peacekeeping had not been a central element of his national security policy during his campaign; he cited it primarily as a way to reduce U.S. security costs.[10] Early statements by administration officials revealed an expansive view toward the subject, however. In April, Secretary of State Christopher said the

---

[10] For example: "We will stand up for our interests, but we will share burdens, where possible, through multilateral efforts to secure the peace, such as NATO and a new, voluntary UN Rapid Deployment force. . . . [t]he UN deserves full and appropriate support from all the major powers. It is time for our friends to bear more of the burden." Speech to the Los Angeles World Affairs Council, August 13, 1992. This emphasis on peacekeeping as burdensharing was echoed in most of Gov. Clinton's other major foreign policy speeches during the campaign. Clinton was guarded in his support of the United Nations as a security institution. For example: "let me be clear: I will never turn over the security of the U.S. to the U.N. or any other international organization. . . . Our motto in this era will be: together when we can; on our own where we must." Speech to the Foreign Policy Association, New York, April 1, 1992.

administration would place "new emphasis on promoting multi-national peace-keeping and peace-making."[11]

Two months later, U.S. Ambassador to the United Nations Madeleine Albright called for "an assertive multilateralism that advances U.S. foreign policy goals."[12] In July, Undersecretary of Defense for Policy Frank Wisner said that peacekeeping "will no longer be an ancillary portion of the thinking of the Department of Defense; it will lie right at the core of our activities in the Office of the Secretary and the Uniformed Armed Forces."[13]

The administration intended to detail its views toward peace-keeping through a formal statement of policy. Just weeks into the new administration, the President issued Presidential Review Directive (PRD) 13, which called on the various national security departments to develop a comprehensive position on peacekeeping policy.[14] Early drafts reportedly "expressed support for 'rapid expansion' of UN operations . . . and committed the United States to support these operations 'politically, militarily, and financially.'"[15]

---

[11] Warren Christopher, "Assistance to Russia and the Foreign Affairs Budget," Statement before the Senate Foreign Relations Committee, April 20, 1993.

[12] Madeleine Albright, Testimony before the Subcommittee on International Security, International Organizations and Human Rights of the House Committee on Foreign Affairs, June 24, 1993.

[13] "International Peacekeeping and Peace Enforcement," Hearing before the Subcommittee on Coalition Defense and Reinforcing Forces of the Committee on Armed Services, July 14, 1993, p. 12.

[14] Some questions about peacekeeping actually were resolved before PRD-13 was even issued. Around the time of the 1992 election, the United Nations Association issued a report on peacekeeping that recommended, among other things, designating U.S. military units to the United Nations for its peacekeeping missions. During the early days of the transition, several members of the advisory committee that oversaw the study—including some who would be appointed to senior national security positions in the new administration—went to review their conclusions with the Chairman of the Joint Chiefs of Staff, General Colin Powell. According to one participant in the meeting: "Powell responded by saying: 'As long as I am Chairman of the Joint Chiefs of Staff, I will not agree to commit American men and women to an unknown war, in an unknown land, for an unknown cause, under an unknown commander, for an unknown duration.' And that was the end of that idea."

[15] Ivo H. Daalder, "The Clinton Administration and Multilateral Peace Operations," Draft case study for the Pew Case Study Program, 1995; Barton Gellman, "Wider U.N. Police Role Supported; Foreigners Could Lead U.S. Troops," *The Washington Post* (August 5, 1993), p. A1.

During early 1993, Congress played little role in the development of peacekeeping policy, appearing content to wait for the
President's review to conclude. The administration conducted no
outreach to members or their staffs as part of the PRD-13
process.[16] The first glimpse of the new policy for most in Congress
was a June 18 *Washington Post* story, which revealed that the
administration's draft policy "would provide for a much wider role
for U.S. military personnel" and noted that the U.S. military had
"agreed to take a case-by-case approach and place U.S. troops under
UN or allied command whenever they find the particular arrangements acceptable."[17] The draft policy approached peacekeeping as
a technical rather than a political question. It barely mentioned
relations with Congress on policy, missions, or funding, except for
a note that war powers issues would be addressed in a separate
review, and that the U.S. should only contribute troops to operations for which public and congressional support could be built.

Although there were a few hearings on peacekeeping and the
issue was raised briefly during several confirmation and general
foreign policy hearings, Congress showed little early inclination
to rein in the activity. Its most significant legislative action was
the passage in both chambers—with almost no debate in the
Senate—of a resolution to authorize the U.S. presence in
Somalia.[18] An administration official noted: "We had a honeymoon. Nobody from Congress was in our face. They had a laissez-
faire attitude. You'd go to Council on Foreign Relations
roundtables on peacekeeping with congressional staff, and they
wouldn't press it."

Events abroad, particularly in Somalia, ended Congress's ret-
icence and the executive's ability to drive peacekeeping policy.

---

[16] Prior to August 8, the President did meet with key members of Congress,
however, to discuss Bosnia and deployed key officials to brief House and Senate
members on the conflict.

[17] R. Jeffrey Smith and Julia Preston, "U.S. Plans a Wider Role in U.N.
Peacekeeping; Administration Drafting New Criteria," *The Washington Post* (June
18, 1993), p. A1.

[18] The measure, Senate Joint Resolution 45, was approved by voice vote in
the Senate on February 4, and by a vote of 243-179 in the House on May 25; the
two chambers never convened a conference committee to reconcile differences
between their respective versions of the bill.

By the time the House considered the Somalia authorization in late May, congressional patience with the operation had begun to ebb. In an early sign of partisanship on peacekeeping, Republicans raised concerns about the operation's cost, purpose, and command arrangements, and voted largely along party lines against the authorization. Then on June 5, soon after the U.S. handed over control of the Somalia operation to the United Nations, forces loyal to Somali warlord Mohammed Farrah Aidid ambushed a UN patrol, killing 24 Pakistani peacekeepers. The Security Council called on UN forces to arrest and punish those responsible for the attack. Operations in Somalia soon resembled combat more than peacekeeping. On August 8, four U.S. soldiers were killed.

In mid-July, Senate Appropriations chair Byrd in a floor speech criticized the expanded U.S. role in Somalia. A month later he warned in *The New York Times* that under the administration's new peacekeeping policy, "we might . . . become militarily involved in operations that the American people don't properly understand or support. . . . Dedication to U.N. Security Council resolutions and peacekeeping missions should not be used by any Administration to escape the hard job of consensus-building in Washington."[19] On September 8, Sen. Byrd introduced a proposal to cut off funding for the U.S. presence in Somalia by the end of October unless Congress authorized the operation. The Senate adopted a non-binding version of the resolution the next day and the House followed suit three weeks later, in both cases by overwhelming margins.

Congressional criticism over the events in Somalia, combined with that of prominent Republicans such as Jeanne Kirkpatrick and Henry Kissinger, led the administration to redraft the policy directive for the President. In place of the initial enthusiasm for peacekeeping, the document emphasized that peacekeeping could advance U.S. national interests in certain circumstances. The initial drafts had included sets of questions the U.S. would press at the United Nations before voting to approve new peacekeeping

---

[19] Robert C. Byrd, "The Perils of Peacekeeping," *The New York Times* (August 19, 1993), p. A23.

missions; the new drafts slightly strengthened these questions. By September 27, in an address to the UN General Assembly, President Clinton's tone was measured: "The United Nations simply cannot become engaged in every one of the world's conflicts. If the American people are to say yes to U.N. peacekeeping, the United Nations must know when to say no."[20]

Congressional dissent already had influenced the administration's tone and policy on peacekeeping. After October 3, however, Congress's assertiveness grew even stronger.[21] The firefight in Mogadishu triggered an explosion of congressional concern and blame-laying. During the following week, there were 67 statements in Congress criticizing the entire Somalia mission or calling for the withdrawal of U.S. troops. On October 5, Secretaries Aspin and Christopher convened a briefing on Somalia for all interested members of Congress; some 200 attended. The bitter and bruising exchange was described by members who attended as "an unmitigated disaster."[22] On October 7, the President and his top national security advisers met at the White House with two dozen of the top leaders in Congress to discuss the crisis—the first meeting between the President and Congress on Somalia—and that evening the President went on television to defend the operation and assure the public that most U.S. forces would be pulled out by March 31.

Despite this assurance, Congress moved quickly to cut off funding for the Somalia operation, although Congress ultimately accepted the President's proposed termination date. The bill con-

---

[20] Address by the President to the 48th Session of the UN General Assembly, New York, September 27, 1993.

[21] October 3 was a turning point for the administration not only on peacekeeping, but on its entire foreign policy and maybe more. Pollster Bill McInturff has noted that the high-water mark in public support for the Clinton health care plan was also October 3. While more immediate factors led to the failure of the Clinton health plan, the debacle in Somalia may have contributed to its demise by dampening public support for the administration and competing for White House attention at a crucial time. Adam Clymer, Robert Pear, and Robin Toner, "For Health Care, Time was a Killer," The New York Times (August 29, 1994), p. A12.

[22] Carroll J. Doherty, "Clinton Calms Rebellion on Hill by Retooling Somalia Mission," Congressional Quarterly (October 9, 1993), p. 2751.

taining these provisions, the annual defense appropriations bill, drew a host of other peacekeeping-related amendments in the Senate. Sen. Don Nickles (R-OK) introduced a measure to restrict the deployment of U.S. troops under foreign command; together with several other Republicans, he argued that the measure was necessary to protect U.S. sovereignty and prevent additional losses of U.S. troops (even though the servicemen killed on October 3 had been under U.S. command). Sen. Dole introduced amendments restricting the deployment of U.S. troops in both Bosnia and Haiti. The Nickles amendment was defeated and the Dole provisions were amended with less restrictive provisions, but only after an intense lobbying effort by top administration officials and the President himself.

By the start of the new year, the administration had redrafted its peacekeeping policy further and was preparing to preview its policy with leading members of Congress. For the first time, the policy now included measures to improve congressional consultation. In part, this addition reflected a decision in October by Ambassador Albright to begin monthly briefings for Congress on upcoming actions at the United Nations.

Before the administration could begin briefings on its new policy, however, Congress again took the initiative. On January 25, Senator Dole published an article announcing his intent to introduce legislation—"The Peace Powers Act"—mandating certain restrictions on peacekeeping and reforms at the United Nations. Among other provisions, the legislation proposed to: prohibit U.S. troops from serving under foreign command; force congressional notification before U.S. votes in the Security Council on peacekeeping operations and before paying UN peacekeeping assessments; require various reports to Congress about peacekeeping operations and budgets; and restrict unreimbursed Pentagon support for peacekeeping operations. After negotiations with the administration, several of these provisions were adopted as part of the State Department's authorization bill.

The administration's peacekeeping policy ultimately was not finalized and issued until May 1994. By then, it had long been overtaken by events and—more important—by Congress. A committee staff director noted: "The final policy was viewed as something that was OK, but somewhat peripheral. It took forever to get it out. By the time it came out, it didn't have a lot to do with the decisions that were going on up on the Hill."

Peacekeeping Funding

While the administration and the press focused throughout 1993 on peacekeeping policy, a less visible battle raged throughout the year over peacekeeping funding. In the end, the debate over money exerted a major influence on policy, and Congress had the upper hand in the funding debate as well.

Problems with funding peacekeeping emerged well before the Clinton administration, as the ending of the Cold War permitted an expansion of peace operations. Peacekeeping had been a minor budget item up through the mid-1980s, averaging about $50 million a year through the decade. As the number of UN peace operations exploded in the late 1980s and early 1990s, however, the costs jumped accordingly for both the United Nations and the United States, which pays about 30 percent of the cost of UN assessed peacekeeping operations.[23] From FY1989 to FY1991, the budget for assessed peace operations more than tripled, from $29 million to $115 million. This figure quadrupled again for FY1992, up to about $460 million. The Bush administration was only able to raise this sum by obtaining supplemental funding during its last year.

---

[23] The United Nations generally creates a separate fund for each peacekeeping operation, but funds them in two different ways. Most peacekeeping operations are "assessed" missions, which means the UN Security Council has voted to apportion its costs among member states. The UN payments formula is based primarily on each nation's income, but permanent members of the Security Council pay a higher rate. The United States pays 30.4 percent of the cost of each operation (compared to a 25 percent rate for the regular UN budget). Although the UN changed its formula in a way that increased the U.S. share to 31.7 percent, the U.S. has refused to pay more than 30.4 percent, and Congress has voted not to pay more than 25 percent beginning in FY1996. Member states also make "voluntary" contributions to peacekeeping operations that are not assessed missions, and through in-kind contributions to other operations. Congress funds these two types of contributions through different subcommittees of its appropriations committees: assessed operations through the CJS appropriations subcommittees, and voluntary contributions through the Foreign Operations subcommittees. Unless otherwise noted, the budget figures cited in this chapter refer only to the U.S. share of assessed operations.

In October 1991, Secretary of State James Baker sent President Bush a memorandum highlighting the divergence between peacekeeping needs and budgets: "With the end of the Cold War, breakthroughs in arms control and planned reductions in the US military presence abroad, we will be turning ever more frequently in the years ahead to the United Nations and to collective defense arrangements. . . . [B]ut with new opportunities and achievements we are being confronted with new financial burdens that far exceed our current ability to pay." Secretary Baker implied that the defense budget should be examined as a source of funds for the soaring peacekeeping bills: "Cambodia and these other peacekeeping operations are far too large to be absorbed within the Function 150 [international affairs] budget cap that is part of the Budget Enforcement Act (BEA), and yet if we do not support them, they risk failure. I recommend that you and I, [OMB Director] Dick Darman and perhaps [Secretary of Defense] Dick Cheney begin to discuss seriously how we are going to respond to peacekeeping funding requirements. . . ."[24]

Indeed, the State Department already was tapping into defense funds to finance peacekeeping. Under the United Nations Participation Act, the Secretary of State is authorized to request Pentagon resources—transport, equipment, personnel, and other goods and services—to support peacekeeping operations. The Secretary of State then can request the Pentagon to waive reimbursement from the United Nations if he deems it in the national interest.[25] In certain circumstances, the State Department can take a credit for these unreimbursed contributions against its outstanding peacekeeping bills. In effect, this process gave administrations a way to use the defense budget to pay part of the UN peacekeeping assessments—an expense nominally funded through the State Department's budget.

A late 1992 State Department memorandum concluded there had been at least 17 times in FY1992 that Foggy Bottom had

---

[24] Memorandum from Secretary of State James Baker to President George Bush, October 3, 1991.

[25] United Nations Participation Act of 1945, PL 79-264, as amended; and Executive Order 10206, of January 19, 1951.

requested peacekeeping support from the Pentagon, ranging from
requests for maps of Cambodia, to calls for C-130s to provide
troop transport to Angola. In nine of these seventeen cases, State
had asked Defense (DoD) to waive reimbursement. The memo
concluded: "DoD has increasingly objected to State's routine
waiver requests, especially where State has separately requested
the UN to credit the value of the unreimbursed DoD assistance
against State's portion of the UN peacekeeping assessment."[26]
The memo proposed the creation of a new DoD account to pay
for the Pentagon's support of peacekeeping—and, where the president thought it in the national interest, to pay for UN peacekeeping assessments.

There were several voices during this period calling for the
Pentagon to pay for *all* peacekeeping costs. In April 1992, Sen.
Paul Simon introduced legislation that proposed to shift funding
for peacekeeping bills to the Defense Department. The bill ultimately attracted 17 co-sponsors, including five Republicans.[27]
Secretary General Boutros-Ghali also had advanced this idea and a
bipartisan Carnegie Endowment commission seconded the proposal.[28] The Senate Armed Services Committee declined to
authorize the change, but it did adopt a provision authorizing up
to $300 million in defense funds to be used to pay UN peacekeep-
ing bills, albeit under quite limited conditions, which were
never met.[29]

The State Department Peacekeeping Account in 1993

The Clinton administration did not initially propose shifting
responsibility for UN peacekeeping bills to the Pentagon. But

---

[26] Undated State Department document, "A Proposal for Enhancing US
Contributions to Peacekeeping: A DoD Fund for Peace," identified by a senior
career official as having been written in the fall of 1992.

[27] The bill was S. 2560.

[28] Boutros-Ghali, op. cit., p. 29; Carnegie Endowment National Commission
on America and the New World, *Changing our Ways* (Carnegie Endowment for
International Peace, 1992), p. 67.

[29] Section 1342, National Defense Authorization Act for FY1993.

from their first days in office, officials in the new administration realized that peacekeeping bills were outstripping their budgets. To meet these escalating costs, the new administration's first budget submission asked for a total of $913 million, almost twice the $460-million budget during the final year of the Bush administration. The new figure included two "add-ons": a supplemental request for $293 million in FY1993 funds; and, as part of the $620 million in FY1994 funds, a contingency fund of $175 million, to be spent on unspecified, unanticipated peacekeeping bills.

Congress rejected both add-ons. The reasons reveal a great deal about relations between the two branches on peacekeeping. The first reason is Congress's general view of the United Nations. Throughout the Cold War, many in Congress saw the institution as a breeding ground for anti-Americanism, anti-Zionism, cronyism, bureaucratic waste, and financial abuse. The institution's ideological overtones became more acceptable to Congress as the Cold War ended, but Congress perceived continuing management problems at the United Nations. In 1985, Congress voted a unilateral reduction in U.S. payments for general UN operations until certain budget reforms were enacted. As the peacekeeping budget grew, Congress attached its reform demands to this account as well.

The second reason for the failure of the 1993 budget proposals relates to the way in which peacekeeping assessments are funded on Capitol Hill. While foreign aid is approved by the Foreign Operations Appropriations Subcommittee, most payments to the United Nations, including those for peacekeeping assessments, fall under the jurisdiction of the Commerce-Justice-State (CJS) Subcommittee. There, the United Nations must compete with domestic programs aimed at crime, immigration, trade promotion, and community economic development. Moreover, many leaders of the CJS subcommittee, such as former House chair Rep. Neal Smith (D-IA) and new chair Rep. Harold Rogers (R-KY), have been strong critics of peacekeeping. As a result, the appropriators often view the peacekeeping account as a source of cuts that can be used to fund domestic needs. As one administration budget official noted, "the 'C' and the 'J' keep eating the 'S.'" In 1993, the appropriators deleted the proposed $175-million contingency fund and reduced the administration's FY1994 peacekeeping request from $620 million to $402 million.[30]

Third, the jurisdiction of CJS over peacekeeping places the account in direct competition with operating funds for the State Department itself, which sometimes tempers State's advocacy on the Hill for the program. In June 1993, the State Department's top management official sent Secretary Christopher a blunt memorandum protesting the cuts that might be required to make the $293-million peacekeeping supplemental viable on the Hill: "If, during a period of continuing cuts to our budget, priority continues to be given to maintaining (in relative terms) discretionary program activities (i.e., incremental policy initiatives) at the expense of our core S & E [salaries and expenses] account, you are going to end up with a hollow State Department. . . . Soon we can close all the posts, rely on CNN, send Executive Level IIIs and above to summits, let the rest of the world pay their way here to see us, and write checks for 'global' programs and peacekeeping."[31] Partly as a result, there was little high-level pressure from the State Department or the White House for the supplemental appropriation for peacekeeping, and it soon died on Capitol Hill.

Fourth, Congress generally does not favor contingency funds. Such funds violate a central premise of congressional oversight: that specific dollars are tied to specific activities. The problem is especially acute for any budget item that is doubling every year or two, as peacekeeping was after 1990. Congress tends to be even more concerned about oversight for activities that could lead to U.S. involvement in military conflicts. Although peacekeeping earlier had been seen as a way to prevent conflict (e.g., Namibia) or avoid direct American involvement (e.g., Cambodia), by 1993

---

[30] For this reason, the Clinton Administration embraced the idea of trying to shift peacekeeping funding from the CJS subcommittee to the Foreign Operations subcommittee. The idea had been previously floated on the Hill by Rep. David Obey, then-chair of the Foreign Operations subcommittee, and rejected by both of the CJS chairs. According to key staff, Rep. Smith rejected the idea because he wanted to retain oversight control of peacekeeping. Sen. Hollings simply said, "Hell no." As a result, the administration found no enthusiasm for the idea and never pushed it.

[31] Memorandum from Undersecretary for Management Richard Moose to Secretary Warren Christopher, June 29, 1993.

Congress began to see peacekeeping as a way the United States could be drawn into foreign quagmires (e.g., Somalia and Bosnia). In this way and many others, funding for peacekeeping is tied up with Congress's war powers, even though the activity is not directly covered by the 1973 War Powers Resolution (unless U.S. troops are involved, and even then only in certain circumstances). Partly for this reason, the House CJS panel not only cut the administration's peacekeeping budget request, it also insisted that Congress be notified in advance before the United States votes for any new peacekeeping missions at the United Nations.

The large cuts sustained in the peacekeeping budget in 1993 further widened the gap between bills and resources. When the President spoke before the UN General Assembly in September that year, he announced: "Within the next few weeks, the United States will be current in our peacekeeping bills." It was true, but only because in early October the administration used virtually the entire peacekeeping appropriation for the coming year to pay its accumulated debts. That action left the United States with almost no resources in 1994 to pay for the many peace operations it continued to support in the Security Council.

Global Cooperative Initiatives

The Clinton administration early on did suggest one idea for funding peacekeeping activities out of the defense budget. In its first budget submission, it proposed that $300 million be provided for the costs of providing troops, goods, and services to support UN peacekeeping operations. This proposal was part of the "Global Cooperative Initiatives" (GCI), which also proposed funds for disaster relief, humanitarian assistance, military-to-military contacts, and similar activities.[32]

The GCI represented an attempt to set aside funds for peace-keeping operations in advance, instead of having funds drawn unpredictably whenever the White House or State Department might call on the military for support. A career Pentagon official explained: "The argument for earmarking these funds was that it would make them pre-planned. We were already funding

---

[32] *Budget of the United States for Fiscal Year 1994*, p. A462.

peacekeeping. The State Department would wheel and deal up in New York and then order DoD to airlift supplies or contribute equipment for various operations. State would credit it against their own bills, and [the services] would never see reimbursement. We would simply take it out of O&M [Operations and Maintenance—the primary operating fund for the services] when the request came. We argued: 'wouldn't it be better to know in advance that this money is coming off the top line, rather than finding out in August that you can't afford to pay for jet fuel, or whatever?'"

Despite the State Department's interest in having the Pentagon share the financial burdens of peacekeeping, the GCI ignited a firestorm between the two departments. State objected that, by authorizing the Secretary of Defense to initiate and oversee peacekeeping, humanitarian, and disaster relief programs, "the proposed legislation would undermine the Secretary of State's ability to carry out his responsibility to coordinate foreign aid-related activities."[33] State said this objection could be overcome only if the Secretary of State had the right to approve each assistance effort under the legislation. The Pentagon objected that such authority would insert the Secretary of State into the military chain of command.

The fight was about more than legal authorities. According to a State Department official: "Everyone viewed it as part of [Defense Secretary Les Aspin's attempt] to set up a mini-State Department." As a result, much as the State Department was eager to unload some of the funding responsibility for peacekeeping onto the much larger Pentagon budget, it was loath to surrender any control. An internal State Department memorandum during this period noted this tension with regard to the idea of shifting all peacekeeping funding to the Pentagon: "IO [State's International Organizations office] believes that, in addition to creating working problems between State and DoD, the transfer of [the peacekeeping account] to the DoD budget would, despite

---

[33] Letter from Assistant Secretary of State for Legislative Affairs Wendy Sherman to OMB Director Leon Panetta, July 1, 1993.

assertions to the contrary, result in a loss of policy control. Peacekeeping funding and policy are inextricably intertwined."[34]

Intense negotiations ensued between the two departments, mediated by the National Security Council, over the degree of oversight each of the two secretaries would have over the funds. As the talks deadlocked in July, officials from each department contacted their respective congressional committees, especially in the Senate, to build political support for their positions. The committee staffs quickly became just as combative. The Senate Armed Services Committee already had marked up its annual authorization bill, and it included the GCI provisions. In an unusual show of muscle, Senate Foreign Relations Committee Chairman Claiborne Pell told Armed Services Chair Sam Nunn he would block the Defense Authorization bill from coming to the Senate floor unless the GCI provisions were stripped. The provisions were deleted.

The GCI was a casualty of a turf war. But even if the State-Defense rift over authorities had been avoided, the GCI might well have failed on Capitol Hill for even more fundamental reasons that touch on the constitutional prerogatives of the executive and Congress. While the GCI was advanced by Pentagon officials as a more rational budgeting method, many on Capitol Hill perceived it as a subtle erosion of Congress's power to exercise oversight of operations that increasingly resembled war. In their view, approving $300 million for unspecified peacekeeping operations might confer tacit congressional approval to the missions themselves. Moreover, the GCI ran contrary to the view, held by many defense legislators and military officials, that the defense budget is meant to pay for *readiness*, not operations. According to a senior staff on one of the Armed Services committees: "The defense budget has never been put together with a view to funding operations aspects with a large price tag. When you get to large operations, that's why you have supplemental

---

[34] Memorandum from Assistant Secretary Robert Gallucci to Undersecretary Peter Tarnoff, May 1, 1993. This tension was not new to the Clinton administration. A Bush State Department official noted: "There were discussions under the Bush administration about using defense money for peacekeeping. We were debating the authorities: Can State take 050 [Defense] money and still decide where it goes?"

appropriations. So GCI was an attempt to pre-fund certain things, and that bothered me a bit." This problem would become clear by September, when the House defeated a proposal to create a far smaller, $30 million fund to pay for the Pentagon's peacekeeping costs, with Republicans calling the fund a "blank check" for the Pentagon.[35]

This problem was understood by a few officials in the Pentagon with congressional experience. One staffer involved in drafting the GCI recalls: "Every time we went to the Comptroller's office, they'd give us these little lectures: 'The defense budget is used to *prepare* the U.S. to fight wars. It's not set up to *do* things. And Congress will never let you do that, because that's Congress's real war power.'" Another says: "We knew we'd be battling a congressional perception that we were creating a 'permission pool.'" Reportedly, Secretary Aspin was aware of this dynamic. Yet the "permission pool" problem was not addressed at the outset with Congress or flagged for the White House. Moreover, the proposal lacked a champion on the Hill because its originator, Morton Halperin, had become embroiled in a fight over his nomination to run a new peacekeeping office within the Pentagon.

Equally important, the GCI ran afoul of concerns among Republicans and conservative Democrats that there was no room in a shrinking defense budget for non-traditional security functions such as peacekeeping. Some centrist House members tried to address both this concern and the desire to protect Congress's war powers prerogatives. During the conference committee on the Defense Appropriations bill, subcommittee chair John Murtha proposed to add a $300-million line item in the defense budget for peacekeeping—but with the stipulations that the figure would be a *ceiling* on such expenditures, and that the administration would have to notify Congress in advance before drawing on the account. The administration rejected the idea as an infringement on the rights of the commander-in-chief. The GCI was dead.

---

[35] Rep. James Hansen (R-UT), quoted in United Nations Association of the United States of America, "House Moves Toward Passage of DoD Authorization," *Washington Weekly Report* (September 24, 1993), p. 2; the amendment was defeated 199-211 on September 10.

Shared Responsibility

By the summer of 1993, the Clinton administration realized it faced a peacekeeping funding crisis. Congress had already signalled its intent to provide less than half of the $913 million that the administration had requested for peacekeeping assessments. At the same time, projections for future bills had climbed since the administration had first submitted its budget. During the spring, the UN operation in Somalia had expanded, and the Security Council had voted to make the UN Protection Force in the Former Yugoslavia an assessed operation. The administration soon realized that, if trends continued, the United States would be $1 billion in arrears on peacekeeping by the end of FY1994.

The arrearages posed several problems for both the United Nations and the United States. The bigger the debts, the longer the United Nations took to pay salaries for troops, the harder it was to get nations to contribute troops, and the more difficult it was for the United States to hand off missions, like Somalia, to the United Nations. The debts also would make it harder for the United Nations to fund the kind of improvements in management of peacekeeping sought by the United States. The debts were a political problem, too. The President was due to address the UN General Assembly in late September; it would be awkward for him to take the podium as the world's biggest peacekeeping debtor.

Some members of Congress recognized the seriousness of the funding crisis and the danger it posed for peacekeeping's future. In August 1993, Foreign Affairs Committee chair Rep. Lee Hamilton wrote to the President urging him to bring together a bipartisan group of key members in order to rally support for paying down the looming arrearages. He urged the President "to put this problem on the level you put the question of aid to Russia, and to make a personal, public appeal for this funding."[36] It would be eight months before such a meeting occurred.

Ultimately, the *funding* problem would sabotage the administration's relations with Congress on peacekeeping *policy*. As one State Department official notes: "We were getting lots of requests

---

[36] Letter from Rep. Lee Hamilton to President Clinton, August 5, 1993.

from the Hill to come up and talk about what was in the presidential review directive. We were told not to do that because funding issues weren't settled. As funding issues dragged out, suspicions grew on the Hill about what was in the presidential directive, and people were able to plant rumors—that it was going to call for sending U.S. troops into more peacekeeping operations, etc. Suspicions and fears grew because they weren't being talked to about it."

In mid-summer 1993, the administration convened a high-level, multi-agency task force on peacekeeping funding. Their recommendation was essentially the same as the one suggested by the State Department under the previous administration: have the Defense Department begin paying some of the assessment bills directly. The concept was dubbed "shared responsibility." It proposed that the State Department still would pay for "traditional" peacekeeping operations—missions under Chapter VI of the UN Charter—when such missions did not include a significant U.S. military presence. However, now the Pentagon would pay for Chapter VI missions involving U.S. troops plus all Chapter VII operations—operations authorized to involve the use of force—whether or not U.S. troops were involved. The department paying the bills for an operation would have lead responsibility within the inter-agency decisionmaking process.

The President's decision directive (portions of which were released to the public) stressed Pentagon expertise as the rationale for shared responsibility: "The military requirements of these operations demand DoD's leadership in coordinating U.S. oversight and management. Professional military judgment increases the prospects of success of such operations. Moreover, with policy management responsibility comes funding responsibility."[37] In reality, however, the driving reason for shared responsibility was budgetary. A State Department official says: "The problem facing the budget task force was that it had to define a way to raid defense without calling it a raid." A Pentagon official offers virtually the same assessment: "Shared responsibility was driven by funding; the question was how to sugar coat the thing."

---

[37] National Security Council, *The Clinton Administration's Policy on Reforming Multilateral Peace Operations*, May 1994, p. 12.

The task force was determined to avoid the GCI experience and preserve comity among the various national security departments. The State Department dropped its resistance to giving the Defense Department more policy control; Pentagon representatives showed a willingness to fund non-traditional expenses. Yet the commitment to collegiality prevented the group from probing some of its assumptions about *Congress's* likely reactions to shared responsibility. One task force member noted: "Everyone left their institutional hats at the door. People were trying to figure out solutions. But it was a bad process in that we never checked on the Hill angle. Shared responsibility was drawn up in a hermetically sealed box. We did it without talking about how we'd involve the Hill and get them on board."

Moreover, the task force accepted the assumption that it would be easier to get Congress to pay for peacekeeping out of the larger Pentagon budget than out of the far-smaller CJS budget. A State Department memorandum from early in the administration had expressed the rationale: "[it is argued by some that] assessed contributions could more easily be made from the National Defense (050) budget function because it is larger than the Foreign Affairs (150) budget function."[38] From Congress's standpoint, however, this was akin to assuming that liver would taste better if part of a bigger meal.

The administration approved the shared responsibility proposal, folded it into its policy directive on peacekeeping, and included $300 million in its proposed FY1995 defense budget to pay for UN peacekeeping assessments. This figure was less than the administration expected would come due on the Pentagon's side of shared responsibility; according to administration officials, it reflected a judgment about the maximum Congress would be willing to fund for the first year of this arrangement.

The proposal immediately ran into trouble in Congress. Despite the support of House Armed Services Committee chair Rep. Ron Dellums (D-CA), members of both parties on the panel voted in March 1994 against using defense funds to pay peace-

---

[38] Memorandum from Principal Deputy Assistant Secretary for International Operations George Ward and Assistant Secretary for Political-Military Affairs Robert Gallucci to Undersecretary Peter Tarnoff, February 1993.

keeping assessments. When the bill reached the floor, a provision was added specifically *prohibiting* any defense funds from being sent to the United Nations.

Shared responsibility received a better reaction in the Senate. Armed Services chair Sen. Sam Nunn approved a proposal by the committee staff to create a new account in the defense budget for paying UN peacekeeping assessments. The provision was more restrictive than the administration's proposal, however. It allowed defense funds to pay for peacekeeping operations that involved US combat forces, but not to fund Chapter VII peace enforcement missions if no U.S. troops participated. This one change knocked out such operations as Somalia (after March 31, 1994) and Bosnia, which accounted for most of the increase in peacekeeping expenses. The bill also required the executive branch to give Congress advance notice before using U.S. combat forces in peace operations and strengthened the Pentagon's ability to get reimbursed by the United Nations.

The provision was reported out in the Committee's bill, although the panel's Republicans voted unanimously against it, and it survived a Republican challenge on the Senate floor. Yet Congress ultimately rejected even this weaker version of shared responsibility. There was growing congressional concern over the impact such a provision could have within a declining military budget. Said one committee staffer: "Anybody reading the tea leaves says: 'hey, $300 million today is $1.1 billion three years from now.'" The House-Senate conference committee deleted the peacekeeping account.

It is tempting to assume that the idea of having the Pentagon pay peacekeeping bills failed due to opposition from the military services. Interviews do suggest that the military's support for the idea (including a call late in the process from the Chairman of the Joint Chiefs of Staff, General Shalikashvili) was tepid. Yet several key staffers in both branches say that it was not the uniformed military but the administration's own political appointees at the Pentagon—several of whom were veterans of the Hill—who weighed in with Congress against shared responsibility. One Pentagon official said: "It was not so much that they didn't like peacekeeping, but they simply thought it did not have much political likelihood of success. They thought that the power chairs, like Murtha and Nunn, would say: 'we don't like this; it isn't home grown; we didn't come up with it.'"

The coolness of Pentagon officials toward shared responsibility was a product not only of the heat they feared they would encounter on the Hill but also of the lack of heat they were sensing from the top of the administration. A meeting between the President and defense legislators planned for May 1994—in part to pitch the importance of shared responsibility—was delayed and then canceled due to conflicts with White House efforts to promote health care reform. One Pentagon official notes the ripple effect that resulted: "The president never touched it. The involvement from the top levels of DoD was half-hearted, sporadic and late. So the legislative people completely didn't push it because it was in the 'too hard' category—it undermined their efforts on their other priorities."

In part, the failure of shared responsibility reveals that administrations must apply consistent pressure, from the president on down, if they hope Congress to accept major changes in national security policies and institutional arrangements—particularly if those changes touch on Congress's constitutional prerogatives. It also suggests that, contrary to what many assumed, it was not easier to fund peacekeeping out of a "big pot" than a "small pot." As part of the defense budget, peacekeeping no longer had to compete with funding for prisons and the Small Business Administration. But it did have to compete with troop salaries and a new aircraft carrier—accounts with massive domestic constituencies of their own and widely accepted security rationales. Given this match-up, no one from the president down to the DoD legislative affairs staff chose to spend much political capital pushing a new Pentagon account for peacekeeping.

The State Department Peacekeeping Account in 1994

While the administration was trying unsuccessfully to obtain Pentagon funding for peacekeeping, it also was working to increase the regular State Department peacekeeping account. The administration's budget proposal for FY1995 requested $1.2 billion for the account, with nearly $1 billion of that (including a proposal for a $670 million FY1994 supplemental appropriation) going for unpaid bills during FY1994 and before. In addition, the budget proposed the new $300-million account in the Defense Department.[39]

The funding proposal got off to a bad start. Soon after the administration's budget request was relayed to the Hill, Congress adopted a package of supplemental appropriations, principally to assist victims of the Los Angeles earthquake, but it declined to include the $670-million supplemental for peacekeeping in the package.

Then two events helped improve prospects for peacekeeping funding. The first was an agreement struck between the executive and Congress as part of the State Department authorization bill, described above. The bill, as it had passed the Senate, included several of the provisions from Sen. Dole's Peace Powers Act, as well as provisions to withhold 20 percent of peacekeeping funds until the United Nations created an inspector general's office. The administration and congressional Democrats agreed to accept these provisions if the bill would endorse the administration's proposal for $670 million in supplemental funding for peacekeeping. The basis of the deal—more congressional money in exchange for more executive accountability—was as old as the Constitution. The bill was sent to the president in late April.

This authorization was helpful, but there was still a question of how to get the funds *appropriated*. For over a year, the administration had tried to identify specific budget cuts in the State Department, the Defense Department, and elsewhere that could be used to pay the mounting pile of peacekeeping bills. Now it tried another approach. It invited the key foreign policy members of Congress from both parties to a breakfast meeting with the President. At the meeting, on April 14, the President explained peacekeeping's financial plight and then asked for ideas on how to fix the problem. Rep. Obey, newly selected as House Appropriations Committee chair, and Senate Appropriations chair Sen. Byrd, suggested a solution. There were small amounts of budget authority "left over" from the previous fiscal year in many of the thirteen Appropriations subcommittees.[40] They proposed

---

[39] *Budget of the United States for Fiscal Year 1995*, pp. 298, 642, 999.

[40] That is, the budget authority used by these subcommittees in the FY1994 funding bills had been less than the budget caps imposed under the budget process to meet annual deficit targets.

reallocating all of these budgetary "remnants" to the CJS subcommittees in order to provide supplemental funding for peacekeeping. Rep. Alan Mollohan (D-WV)—the new House CJS chairman and more supportive of peacekeeping than his predecessor, Rep. Neal Smith—strongly endorsed the idea.[41]

After all the congressional animosity toward peacekeeping over the previous year, this was an extraordinary offer of help—particularly on the part of Sen. Byrd, who had been one of peacekeeping's fiercest critics in Congress. One Senate Appropriations staffer notes: "I never thought in a million years we'd do what we did: reallocate funds from the other subcommittees—Defense, Labor/HHS—to pay for peacekeeping. This was money the other subcommittees could have used."

Several factors explain the response. First, many in Congress perceived that what was at stake was not funding for *future* peacekeeping, but bills for *past* peacekeeping; thus, they saw fewer questions of war powers or congressional oversight at stake. As one of Sen. Byrd's staff notes, "the argument that these were debts owed resonated with Sen. Byrd; he has said we shouldn't be supporting these large budgets for the UN, but we do have to pay these debts we've accrued." Second, this was the first time the President had personally asked for Congress's help in paying for peacekeeping. A key Senate aide noted: "the personal request at the breakfast was important—personal relations around here matter a lot." Third, restrictions passed in the State Authorization bill, and the administration's more guarded tone toward peacekeeping since September 1993, eased congressional worries about excessive reliance on the United Nations. Fourth, many of the appropriators realized that if they did not address the peacekeeping debts in this way, they might need to pass a supplemental bill later that would increase the deficit, which would be even worse politically.

---

[41] Mollohan's assumption of this chairmanship, as well as the elevation of Rep. Obey to chairmanship of the full House Appropriations committee, occurred following the death of Rep. William Natcher (D-KY) in March 1994. Rep. Smith lost to Rep. Obey in the race to replace Natcher; Smith instead assumed chairmanship of the subcommittee on Labor, Health and Human Services, and Education.

Once the key members had reached agreement, the CJS bill moved relatively smoothly. The House bill moved from the subcommittee to approval on the floor in June. It funded the entire administration request of $1.2 billion, including the $670 million supplemental appropriation. The package was assisted on the House floor by a letter, signed by several pro-defense legislators, endorsing the peacekeeping funds. Part of their motivation was reportedly to reduce the likelihood that defense funds would be tapped for peacekeeping bills. The Senate Appropriations committee approved virtually the same amount in mid-July. The funding package ran into a political buzz saw on the Senate floor, however, when Republicans pushed through an amendment to delete $350 million from peacekeeping and to use it instead to reimburse the states for the costs of incarcerating illegal aliens. The amendment drew disproprotionately strong support from Senate freshmen, with a roughly 20 percentage point gap in each party between freshmen and non-freshmen. However, after strong administration lobbying—OMB Director Panetta called peacekeeping the administration's top priority in the CJS bill—the provision was deleted in the conference committee. In August, both Houses approved the full $1.2 billion appropriation.

Epilogue

Despite the success of the 1994 CJS bill, congressional resistance to peacekeeping quickly resumed. The President's controversial military occupation of Haiti in September 1994—without congressional support or authorization—spurred more congressional objections over the use of U.S. troops and Pentagon resources for essentially humanitarian missions. The continuing inability of UN peacekeepers to stem aggression in the former Yugoslavia raised further congressional objections against the United Nations and its peacekeeping capacities.

Although the budget submitted by the Clinton administration in early 1995 once again proposed over $1 billion for peacekeeping assessments, including a renewed request for a peacekeeping account at the Pentagon, the new Republican Congress seemed certain to restrict peacekeeping funding and policy significantly. Midway through its first 100 days in session, the House adopted most of the peacekeeping provisions in the GOP's Contract with America. One part of the House bill would, in essence, reduce U.S. peacekeeping payments to the United Nations by any extra costs the Pentagon had incurred supporting UN peacekeeping missions—a range of activities estimated to total $1.7 billion in 1994.[42] Legislation introduced by Senate Majority Leader Dole contained similar language. Secretary of State Christopher and Secretary of Defense William Perry argued that such provisions could shut down UN peacekeeping, and the bill drew the administration's first veto threat on a piece of national security legislation.

As these provisions awaited Senate consideration, the determination of the Republican Congress to assert itself on peacekeeping was clear. As the House passed its provisions, Rep. Toby Roth (R-WI) said, "What we're saying in this part of the Contract with America is that Congress must be more involved."[43]

---

[42] Pat Towell, "House Votes to Sharply Rein In U.S. Peacekeeping Expenses," *Congressional Quarterly* (February 18, 1995), p. 537.

[43] Eric Schmitt, "House Votes Bill to Cut U.N. Funds for Peacekeeping," *The New York Times* (February 17, 1995), p. A1.

4 Conclusions

The 1993 Russia/NIS aid package and peacekeeping policy during 1993-94 are vivid examples of the divided picture in current executive-congressional relations on national security. Congress was energetically cooperative with the executive on the first, fiercely resistant on the second. With the arrival of a Republican Congress in 1995, the level of rancor between the two branches generally has escalated. Yet the White House and Congress remain more constructive on some national security issues than others, and the two cases in the preceding chapters offer some insights about why and when cooperation is most likely to occur.

What explains the differences between the two cases? Some will argue that the administration simply lacked commitment and competence in making the case for peacekeeping. They will contend that if it had put as much muscle behind its peacekeeping initiatives as it applied to assistance for Russia and the other NIS, Congress would have agreed to both. This answer is unsatisfying. The 1993 Russia/NIS aid package often continued to move ahead *despite* major administration missteps, such as the failure to consult with Congress before announcing a sixfold increase in aid. In contrast, the administration's peacekeeping initiatives often failed to advance *even with* high-level pressure, such as the effort mounted in 1994 to create a peacekeeping account at the Pentagon. Competence only explains so much. It is important to ask: Were there things about an aid package for Russia and the NIS that predisposed Congress to be receptive? Is there something about peacekeeping that engenders opposition, especially from Republicans and conservative Democrats? Are there qualities of each issue that explain the amount of muscle the administration used to sell them on Capitol Hill?

This chapter attempts to identify the factors that account for the different fates of the two initiatives on Capitol Hill. It concludes that the outcomes were determined both by the nature of the issues involved and the pattern of the executive branch's outreach to Congress. It suggests that while Congress is becoming relatively more assertive, its assertiveness is uneven, and the same factors that differentiated the outcomes on these two case studies are likely to do so for other national security issues as well. A closing section offers some recommendations for improving executive-congressional relations on national security in the coming years.

Factors that Shape the Success of Executive Branch Proposals

This study's opening chapter argued that, after a major war, whether the executive branch emerges stronger or weaker on national security affairs relative to the Congress tends to depend on a specific set of factors: perceptions of the postwar threat; perceptions of the war just ended; the state of the economy after the war; and the executive branch's management of its relations with Congress, particularly the extent of its bipartisan outreach. Since these variables appear to explain how relations between the branches generally change over a period of years, we should also expect to discern them at work in determining whether particular executive branch initiatives engender congressional cooperation or opposition.

In fact, a comparison of the two cases in this study shows that roughly the same factors—plus one other—explain most of the differences in how the two initiatives fared in Congress. While it would require analysis of additional case studies and congresses to prove the point, we can speculate that for some time to come the executive branch is likely to gain congressional cooperation on specific security initiatives depending on how they stand up to the following questions:

1. Are high national security stakes involved?
2. Does the issue resemble Cold War concerns?
3. Is the initiative likely to produce domestic economic benefits?
4. How intensively does the executive branch manage its congressional relations, including bipartisan outreach?

5. Does the initiative avoid areas of constitutional disagreement between the branches, such as that over war powers?

These central factors are of course to some extent interdependent. The scale of the national security stakes, for example, can affect how likely the executive branch is to reach out to both parties in Congress. Conversely, the extent of an administration's bipartisan outreach can change perceptions about an initiative's national security stakes. While the relationships among these factors are complex, each factor exerts some independent influence, and it is useful to consider each in some depth.

1. *High national security stakes.* The most important difference between the two case studies examined was the degree to which Congress perceived clear and sizable security interests to be at stake. The judgment is obviously subjective; what is vital to one person may be peripheral to another. Yet the statements of members of Congress on the floor and in interviews for this study yield distinctly different perspectives of the security interests involved in Russia/NIS assistance and in peacekeeping. For example, asked to explain why Congress was willing to use defense funds for the former but not the latter, one Senator on a defense panel responded: "People feel more strongly that the survival of Yeltsin and [Russian] democracy are important to our security than the ability of the UN to run military operations." Or, put in the terms Sen. Vandenberg used with President Truman: you can "scare the hell out of the country" over Russia, but not over Somalia, Bosnia, or Haiti.

In the case of the Russia/NIS package, members of Congress perceived the security stakes in vivid, compelling terms. For example, during the House debate, then-Minority Whip Gingrich concluded: "we have a chance today to do what we can to make the world safer so our sons and daughters do not die in a war and so our cities are not incinerated."[1] Members found that the package survived the acid test: Constituents supported it despite a general aversion to foreign aid. A conservative Republican Representative said, "my voters understood the military argument—like the case for the Nunn-Lugar funds—and I could also

---

[1] *Congressional Record* (June 17, 1993), p. H3745.

make the case well when I was asked about why it's worth assisting Russia in other ways. People understood." Because of the large security risks involved, a vote for the administration's package also provided political cover if the situation in Russia did turn sour. A senior administration official notes: "We were covering *their* [Congress's] behind. They were buying an insurance policy. If there was a debate over who lost Russia, they couldn't be blamed. You couldn't lose on this vote."

On peacekeeping, in contrast, members of Congress discounted the security rationale. A Republican House committee chairman says, "the conflict [over peacekeeping] is about what constitutes the national interest when you get into these peripheral areas of conflict." Especially after the Somalia deployment—but well before the firefight on October 3 in Mogadishu—Congress began to equate "peacekeeping" with "humanitarian." During the May 1993 House debate over the resolution authorizing the U.S. troop presence in Somalia, the ranking Republican member of the Foreign Affairs committee, Rep. Benjamin Gilman (R-NY) said: "in this effort, no vital American interests are at stake that require any long-term American troop peacekeeping presence. . . . With new peacekeeping operations demanding additional resources and commitments from the United States, we need to begin to set realistic and feasible limits on our *humanitarian* commitments around the world."[2] The very presence of "national security interest waivers" in many of the restrictions Congress has proposed on peacekeeping recently— such as on foreign command of U.S. troops—suggests that members doubt national security is usually at risk in such operations.

The difference in national security stakes helps answer a fundamental question: Why have some national security issues, such as peacekeeping, turned partisan, while others, such as the Russia/NIS aid package in 1993, have risen above partisanship? National security proposals tend to become divided along partisan lines when they play into a broader critique of one of the parties (usually the one occupying the White House) *and* when members perceive relatively little security risk to the nation in the propos-

---

[2] *Congressional Record* (May 25, 1993), pp. H 2748, H 2754; emphasis added.

al's possible defeat. Both Russian aid and peacekeeping potential-
ly bolstered long-standing Republican critiques of the Democratic
party: on Russia, that Democrats through the late Cold War had
been naive about Moscow; on peacekeeping, that Democrats
overemphasize moral and humanitarian concerns relative to
"hard" security matters and often rely on multilateral bodies such
as the United Nations to the detriment of U.S. national interests.
Yet the 1993 package of aid for Russia and the other NIS never
drew such partisan attacks; the reason appears to be that members
of Congress perceived enormous security consequences for the
United States if the reform movements in the Soviet successor
states failed. Members had to worry about the political price they
might pay in a debate over "who lost Russia?," but few had to fear
a debate over "who lost Rwanda?" Indeed, Republican members
had something to gain in a debate over "who lost American lives
and military readiness for humanitarian interventions?"[3]

Similarly, the difference in security stakes helps explain the
difference in how the two initiatives moved through the legislative mill. Because members readily grasped the security rationale
for Russia/NIS aid, administration missteps with Congress did not

---

[3] A related question, beyond the scope of this study is: How do the votes of
individual members of Congress on these issues relate to public opinion? As
noted, the expansion of aid to Russia in 1993 succeeded despite public opposition,
while peacekeeping became increasingly unpopular in Congress despite strong
public support. Some have suggested that Congress simply misperceives public
opinion, particularly on peacekeeping. For example, based on their public opinion
polling, summarized in Chapter 3, Steven Kull and Clay Ramsay write: "Why is
there such a widespread impression that the public is of an isolationist bent and
opposed to spending money on UN peacekeeping when, apparently, this is not the
case? One possible reason is that the public is comfortable with this image of
itself as isolationist and therefore does not resist it when it is presented in the
media and by policymakers." *U.S. Public Attitudes on UN Peacekeeping*
(Program on International Policy Attitudes, March 1994), p. 15. An alternative
hypothesis—which this study tends to support—is that Congress is only likely to
support national security initiatives based solely on moral or humanitarian
grounds to the extent such issues generate organized or grassroots support. For
example, popular revulsion against apartheid generated sufficient interest group
and grassroots opposition to overwhelm the security arguments posed by the
Reagan administration for "constructive engagement." The United Nations and
peacekeeping, while broadly supported in polls, do not seem to generate much
pressure by interest groups or voters in support, while they do excite the energies
of the smaller number of citizens who deeply oppose these programs. What may
be important to members of Congress is not aggregate public opinion about a vote
but rather the heat it is likely to generate.

doom the proposal. The administration's failure to notify key members before announcing the sixfold increase in aid irritated them but did not lessen their ability to line up support. On peacekeeping, in contrast, members did not feel that sufficient arguments existed to overcome the resistance of defense legislators, UN skeptics, and partisan Republicans. Only White House pressure seemed to move the issue. When that pressure was absent or misapplied, the perception of low national security stakes ensured that progress on the peacekeeping initiatives would stall. Ultimately, it may be that the administration would have needed to spend more effort advocating its peacekeeping initiatives in Congress, if they were to succeed, than it devoted to its Russia/NIS aid proposal. Yet, as discussed below, precisely because the security stakes were lower for peacekeeping, the administration was reluctant to devote such a high level of political resources.

Nowhere was this difference clearer than in the actions of Sen. Byrd, who played a decisive role in each case. On assistance for Russia and the NIS, Sen. Byrd was determined to help his party's president, even if it meant stretching the 1990 budget deal that was so important to him (by putting the reserves for the Israeli loan guarantees off budget). On peacekeeping, however, Sen. Byrd opposed his party's president and only agreed to a major funding package in 1994 because the President asked him personally, and because he feared that *failing* to provide the funds in 1994 would require increasing the deficit later.

If Congress tends to defer when the national security stakes are high, that does not mean the two branches are destined to clash on every issue with low national security stakes. There are innumerable minor issues and programmatic details on which Congress and the executive branch happen to hold similar views. Yet the more both branches perceive the security of the country to be at stake, the more the executive branch will be able to overcome the political and financial constraints—deficits, domestic needs, wariness of new foreign entanglements—that arise after major wars and that confront the nation now.

2. *Resemblance to Cold War concerns.* Chapter 1 argues that perceptions of the war just completed help change the balance of power between the branches. One way such perceptions exert an influence is by providing a framework for understanding new security challenges in a postwar period. For example, in his 1947 address to Congress, President Truman sought to cast the Cold War in World War II terms: "One of the primary objectives of the foreign policy of the United States is the creation of conditions in which we and other nations will be able to work out a way of life free from coercion. This was a fundamental issue in the war with Germany and Japan."[4] One of the reasons the Russia/NIS package succeeded was that the public and Congress could understand it within the framework of the Cold War. The same was not true for peacekeeping.

Aid to post-communist states might be a new issue for Congress; Russia was not. Long years of Cold War experience left members of Congress agreeing on the seriousness of the consequences should Russia plunge into chaos or revert to imperialism. Indeed, key elements of the package, such as housing for Russian troops withdrawing from the Baltics, were directly linked to Cold War objectives. One conservative Representative thus described the 1993 bill as a way of "putting some neat wrapping" around the Cold War.

Ironically, Congress had many more years of experience with peacekeeping than with aid to former communist states. The United States had first contributed military personnel to UN peace operations during the organization's first observer mission in Palestine in 1948. Yet peacekeeping's advocates were hard-pressed to link their cause to the recent victory in the Cold War. Indeed, President Clinton's policy announcement on the issue noted how *little* peacekeeping played a role in the Cold War: "During the Cold War, the United Nations could resort to multilateral peace operations only in the few cases when the interest of the Soviet Union and the West did not conflict."[5] The inability of peacekeeping advocates to portray their issue as a logical extension of the nation's Cold War efforts made it harder for them to build political support for the program.

3. *Promise of domestic economic benefits.* After a war and the economic downturn that typically follows, the American people and

---

[4] Truman, *op. cit.*

[5] National Security Council, *The Clinton Administration's Policy on Reforming Multilateral Peace Operations*, May 1994, p. 1.

their representatives in Washington naturally clamor for legislation to improve the domestic economy. Foreign policy initiatives are hard-pressed to compete with domestic programs unless they can lay claim to domestic economic benefits.

The Russia/NIS aid package was designed and marketed to Congress in a way that emphasized domestic economic benefits. The administration placed heavy emphasis on trade and agricultural assistance. President Clinton's first statement in office arguing for an increase in Russia/NIS aid was an address about the importance of foreign programs in fueling America's economic renewal.[6] In that speech and others that followed, he stressed two domestic economic benefits: the ability to maintain lower defense budgets as long as Russia remained peaceful, and the long-run potential for increased trade with Russia and other former communist states. It soon became clear there were other domestic economic benefits to the package: a *Wall Street Journal* article in 1994 revealed that 50-90 percent of many aid contracts funded by the bill were going to U.S. business and media consultants.[7]

Such economic benefits were stressed repeatedly in Congress's floor debates on the package. For example, during the House debate Rep. Hyde argued: "[The bill offers an opportunity] to turn what have been 300 million enemies into 300 million customers . . . Access to oil, to natural gas, to rare metals, to minerals, they have a boundless amount of them over there, and when we become trading partners instead of adversaries, the benefits will be incalculable. . . ."[8]

Virtually none of these domestic economic benefits were associated with peacekeeping. Peacekeeping assessments are sent to the United Nations, which spends a large share of the money to pay foreign troops. Although the available data suggests that U.S. vendors receive over a third of UN peacekeeping expenditures for supplies and services, Congress saw the glass as two-thirds empty and passed language implying that American vendors had been

---

[6] Remarks by the President at American University Centennial Celebration, February 26, 1993.

[7] John J. Fialka, "U.S. Aid to Russia is Quite a Windfall—For U.S. Consultants," *The Wall Street Journal* (February 24, 1994), p. A1.

[8] *Congressional Record* (June 17, 1993), p. H 3743.

treated unfairly.[9] Finally, although the primary argument for peacekeeping from the Clinton administration and other supporters was that it offered the United States a way to save money, this argument rang hollow as peacekeeping assessments increased tenfold in just four years (FYs 1991-1995).

The economy shaped both of the case studies in one other important way. They were both constrained by the deficit. In both cases, efforts to obtain "emergency" supplemental funds—that is, funds financed by increasing the deficit—died quickly. Both the sixfold increase in funds for Russia and the NIS in 1993 and the largest-ever package of peacekeeping money in 1994 were financed in appropriations bills that were smaller than the previous year's bills and within deficit reduction targets for the year. Congress's aversion to new spending on foreign ventures was clear from its floor debates. In the House debate on the Russia/NIS aid package, for example, Rep. Obey stressed to his colleagues: "Not one dime of aid to the Soviet Union is coming out of any program to help people here at home. This program is being funded by reductions in our other foreign aid accounts and by taking almost $1 billion out of the military budget."[10]   As the 104th Congress begins its work, deficit pressures as much as security arguments have been behind budget proposals that would reduce funding for both Russia and peacekeeping—as well as most other international accounts.

4. The executive branch's management of its relations with Congress on the issue. National security initiatives do not sell themselves in Congress, no matter how high the security stakes and economic benefits. The experiences of Presidents Wilson, Truman and Clinton—as well as many others—suggest that the executive branch's management of its relations with Congress matters. In

---

[9] Department of State, "Summary of United Nations Procurement for Peacekeeping—1993," attachment to certification letter on peacekeeping from Deputy Secretary Strobe Talbott to Senator Ernest Hollings, October 13, 1994. The document notes that the United Nations only has data on vendor payments by country for two categories of peacekeeping costs, commercial procurement by the New York headquarters, and "letters of assist" used for procurement directly from member states because of the urgency or unique nature of the good or service needed. The dollar-share of these two categories going to U.S. vendors was 28 percent and 51 percent, respectively; the dollar-weighted total for both categories was 36 percent. No data was available for local procurement by field missions.

[10] *Congressional Record* (June 17, 1993), p. H 3742.

particular, in proposing a national security initiative to Congress, it matters whether the executive branch reaches out to both parties, clearly identifies the proposal as a priority, and deploys powerful champions to advocate the idea. The executive did all three to build support for the Russia/NIS aid package. There was little comparable effort on peacekeeping.

As Chapter 2 details, key officials in both Congress and the executive branch decided early on that obtaining expanded assistance for Russia and the other NIS would require bipartisan cooperation. The President began lobbying members of Congress of both parties, at the White House dinners and through other means, long before announcing the package. Certainly it was helpful that assistance to Russia and the NIS had enjoyed the support of the preceding Republican administration. Yet without deliberate efforts by many of those involved to reinforce existing support on both sides of the aisle, it is not clear that the bipartisan coalition for Russia/NIS aid would have endured. President Yeltsin's March 20 declaration of extra-constitutional powers and the disbanding of Parliament on September 21 both came at crucial times; both could have fueled Republican arguments against the package. A senior Clinton administration official notes the uncertain atmosphere that prevailed in the spring of 1993: "There was a potential for partisan differences. Yeltsin hadn't won on the streets. Some urged us to be more cautious." The wide, bipartisan margins by which the legislation passed were not inevitable.

The administration also clearly communicated to Congress and the public the high priority that President Clinton placed on the aid initiative. Within days of his inauguration, the President tagged Russia and the other NIS as his "number one" foreign policy priority, gave major speeches laying out the case for the aid package, and brought key members of Congress to the White House to ensure they heard the message. Moreover, the administration was unwavering in its commitment to the proposal, even in the face of disruptions at home and in Russia.

The administration reenforced these messages by deploying powerful champions in support of the proposal. The President, Secretary of State Christopher and National Security Adviser Anthony Lake all weighed in with Congress early and often.

Ambassador Talbott spoke extensively with members of Congress, and they understood he was speaking for his close friend, the President. Secretary of Defense Aspin, who had been an early proponent of using defense funds for assisting Russia, stressed his support for the bill. All of these executive branch signals helped bolster Congress's own long-time champions of assistance to the former Soviet Union, such as Majority Leader Gephardt, Rep. Obey, and Sen. Nunn.

Peacekeeping, in contrast, enjoyed almost none of these advantages. There was little high-level outreach to congressional Republicans until late in the game. The President's first meeting on Somalia with the Congress's bipartisan leadership occurred only after the October 3 firefight. The administration's first staff-level briefings for members of both parties on its new peacekeeping policy did not occur until January 1994, and it was not until April of that year that the President met with bipartisan leaders to make the direct case for extra peacekeeping funding.

There also was little effort by the administration to declare peacekeeping a top priority until early 1994. Whereas discussions on policy toward Russia and the other NIS began immediately and at the highest level, the peacekeeping review—like dozens of other policy reviews initiated by the new administration—was delegated to the assistant-secretary level or lower and put on a brisk but hardly urgent schedule. Whereas the President made major statements about aid to Russia and the NIS during his second and fourth months in office, he did not make any major statements about peacekeeping until his ninth month in office. Although the administration asked for a contingency fund and a supplemental appropriation for peacekeeping in its 1993 budget, it mounted no high-level effort to obtain them. The administration allowed its first major innovation in peacekeeping funding—Global Cooperative Initiatives—to become mired in inter-department wrangling. Congress noted all these signals and concluded peacekeeping was not a top priority, at least for 1993.

Finally, while the Russia/NIS aid package enjoyed powerful champions, peacekeeping was a policy orphan. The Secretary of State did not place peacekeeping on his list of top priorities. His top management people tempered their advocacy for peacekeeping in part because it was in competition with State's operating expenses. The top advocates for peacekeeping at both the State Department and the Pentagon were at the assistant-secretary level—and at the Pentagon, the assistant secretary-designate was embroiled in a losing confirmation fight, in part over this issue. Several political appointees in the Pentagon actively undermined some of the administration's own peacekeeping initiatives, and the military was often cool to the program. The most powerful executive branch champion, Ambassador Albright, was 200 miles away from Washington.

Due to all of these factors, peacekeeping ultimately had even fewer powerful champions in Congress. The chairs of the relevant appropriations subcommittees were leading critics (at least until early 1994, when Rep. Mollohan replaced Rep. Smith). The chairs of the foreign affairs authorizing committees liked peacekeeping; however, given the decline in these committees over the past three decades, they could deliver few dollars or votes. Apart from a few exceptions, such as Rep. Dellums, defense legislators were strongly critical of peacekeeping. Sen. Nunn was willing to fight for a weak version of the administration's shared-responsibility initiative in 1994, but it was hardly his top priority. The only time heavyweight congressional champions surfaced for peacekeeping was in 1994, as the titans of the appropriations committees decided to use leftover funds to pay for peacekeeping debts. Even then there was little enthusiasm. The full committee chairs saw it as the only way to avoid an "emergency," deficit-increasing bill. Key defense legislators saw it as a way to avoid raids on Pentagon funds. On Russian aid, Majority Leader Gephardt had organized a congressional delegation to Russia to bolster bipartisan support; peacekeeping, having no comparable champions to launch similar strategies, was left defenseless when it started to come under partisan—and often, bipartisan—attack.[11]

---

[11] To the extent that Congress proved more willing to fund peacekeeping in 1994, it was partly because the administration sent signals that proved it had become a higher priority. The President met with key members of Congress. OMB Director Panetta and other senior administration officials lobbied the Hill for the funds. Panetta told the CJS panel that peacekeeping funding was the administration's "number one priority" in their appropriations bill—even as crime programs, also funded out of the same pot, were heating up as a political issue for the 1994 elections.

These points demonstrate that an administration's advocacy of an initiative can change congressional perceptions about the proposal's merits, energize congressional advocates, and silence potential opponents. It is also true, however, that perceptions about an issue's importance influence how an administration apportions its limited political capital in its relations with Congress. The Russia/NIS aid package and peacekeeping demonstrate the point. The two initiatives were not just contrasts when it came to executive branch advocacy. They were also competitors. The administration, believing that relations with Russia and the other NIS were more important for national security than peacekeeping, repeatedly chose to use its congressional chits for the former at the expense of the latter. One administration official responsible for peacekeeping said: "When the money problem started to become evident [in May 1993], we were told: 'shut up—we can't raise that with the Hill now because of Russian aid.'" The conflict persisted until the Russian aid bill had cleared the Congress. An August 1993 memorandum from the State Department's legislative director cautioned that by raising peacekeeping policy and funding on the Hill, "we may put at risk another Administration priority, Russian aid. We will almost certainly be asked by Congress: 'What is your priority? Russian aid or peacekeeping?'"[12]

5. Avoidance of areas of constitutional disagreement between the branches. One of the most decisive differences between the two case studies was the degree of controversy over the constitutional prerogatives of the two branches. The "invitation to struggle" that Corwin described applies to some national security issues more than others. Congress rarely has challenged the President's authority to direct the conduct of a war. The executive branch rarely has questioned Congress's right to conduct oversight hearings as it funds specific programs. But there are many policy casualties in the battle zone of constitutional ambiguity, particularly on war powers questions. Aid to Russia and the NIS stood safely outside that battle zone. Peacekeeping was—and remains—ground zero.

---

[12] Memorandum from Assistant Secretary of State Wendy Sherman to the Deputy Secretary; undated, but probably August 1993.

In the case of aid to Russia and the NIS, the division of executive-congressional labor was clear, and it fit well with each branch's views of its own duties and prerogatives. The administration conducted the diplomacy, drew the broad outlines of its program, declared a goal in the form of a dollar figure, and made the case to the public. Congress figured out how to fund the package and get it passed. The most contentious issue of executive-congressional prerogatives involved designating funds for Ukraine and Armenia; even on these, the executive branch ultimately met or exceeded the amounts that Congress prescribed with non-binding language.

Peacekeeping, in contrast, has become the primary arena for constitutional disagreement between the two branches in national security policy. Congress has come to view peacekeeping as it once saw foreign military assistance: the camel's nose that could lead U.S. troops into the tent of foreign fighting. Concerns over UN management and the 20-fold increase in UN peacekeeping costs over the past decade would be enough to trigger Congress's oversight concerns. But the increasing association of peacekeeping with U.S. casualties—from Beirut to Mogadishu—has led Congress to assert its war powers as well.

The Clinton administration saw policy, not inter-branch disagreements, as the most pressing question to settle on peacekeeping. But in trying to put out the policy fires among its agencies, the administration ignored a constitutional back draft that was waiting to explode with Congress. The biggest administration success on peacekeeping—raising $1.2 billion in the 1994 CJS bill for UN assessments—came in part because the constitutional issues were muted: the main issue was paying the bills for past UN missions rather than continuing existing ones or getting into new ones.

Implications for Future Relations Between the Branches

These factors suggest why relations between the two branches were so different on the 1993 Russia/NIS aid package and the peacekeeping initiatives of 1993-94, and they suggest the kinds of national security issues on which the executive branch is most likely to prevail in Congress. More important, these factors suggest two general conclusions about the behavior and power of the two branches on national security in the coming years.

First, the pivotal factor in most major national security debates is likely to be the qualities of the issue at hand rather than partisanship; indeed, the qualities of the issue at hand are likely to determine whether the debate becomes partisan. That is, contrary to most current commentary, the rise of a Republican Congress will not bring across-the-board changes on national security votes. Undoubtedly, the new partisan mix will change the *tenor* of interbranch debates. There will inevitably be a decline in the percentage of contested votes that the Clinton administration wins in Congress during the next two years, and the President may well exercise his veto for the first time on national security legislation. But the degree of partisan rancor and the outcomes on major initiatives continue to hinge heavily on such factors as the level of national security stakes and the degree of domestic benefits involved.

For example, despite a more confrontational tone, Congress may well remain relatively cooperative on such administration proposals as aid to former communist states, the expansion of NATO membership, and China's trade status. In contrast, this analysis suggests the administration is likely to fare poorly on contested proposals regarding Bosnia, foreign aid, the global environment, population programs and peacekeeping—areas where the national security stakes are not widely accepted or low.

Support for this thesis comes from the early attitude of Republicans in the 104th Congress toward the October 1994 accord that the United States signed with North Korea regarding the latter's nuclear program. Several prominent Republicans attacked the accord after it was signed. Soon after the November elections, however, Senator Frank Murkowski (R-AK), who had been the ranking Republican of the subcommittee on Asia, traveled to Pyonyang along with Sen. Paul Simon (D-IL) to assess the accord. Sen. Murkowski came away less critical of the agreement, reporting that he and Simon "saw, repeatedly, affirmative commitment on the part of North Korea to live up to their part of the deal," and concluding that the new Republican majority was unlikely to scuttle the deal.[13]

---

[13] T. R. Reid, "Visiting Senators Learn Little of N. Korean Leader; Since Father's Death, Kim Keeps Low Profile," *The Washington Post* (December 13, 1994), p. A32.

Former Secretary of State Baker reenforced this view in January when he told members of the House International Relations Committee: "Do I think that you ought to step in and somehow through the power of the purse foreclose the ability of the United States to perform on the agreement? I really don't [because] then you're taking on your shoulders the responsibility for what might happen if the United States unilaterally walked away from an agreement it has negotiated with North Korea."[14] As this study goes to press, the House appears poised to approve legislation that would restrict funding for elements of the accord. Yet President Clinton has threatened a veto, partly over these provisions, and the analysis in this study suggests that, while congressional Republicans are likely to criticize the agreement, they are also likely to leave the administration with broad discretion.

A second conclusion of this study is that, barring the emergence of some major new threat to American security, Congress is likely to be somewhat more powerful in inter-branch relations than it was during much of the late-Cold War period. Clearly, the power of the executive will increase whenever the president and the majorities in the House and Senate all come from the same political party, as was the case over the past two years. But apart from these partisan fluctuations, Congress is likely to be more resistant to presidential leadership than it was, say, during the early 1980s.

Chapter 3 shows how the post-Cold War Congress has been more assertive on issues such as peacekeeping, on which it perceives the security stakes to be low. But there are factors other than the loss of an overarching security threat eroding the executive branch's power. Party leaders and foreign policy elites have less control over freshmen and other junior members. As was evident with peacekeeping, blurring definitions of "security" tend to spur fights among executive branch agencies—especially the Departments of State and Defense—which can weaken the president's ability to sell national security initiatives to the Congress.[15]

---

[14] Hearing of the House International Relations Committee, January 12, 1995.

[15] Randall B. Ripley and James M. Lindsay predict increased congressional activism on national security policy due to some similar factors in "Foreign and Defense Policy in Congress: an Overview and Preview," in Ripley and Lindsay, ed., *Congress Resurgent: Foreign and Defense Policy on Capitol Hill* (University of Michigan Press, 1993), pp. 13-14.

As a result, there are early signs that, after the end of the Cold War, the executive branch is having difficulty in getting its way even when an administration claims the national security stakes to be very significant. The most notable example came at the start of 1995, when resistance from the 104th Congress forced President Clinton to modify his proposed package of financial assistance for Mexico.

As the peso lost roughly a third of its value relative to the dollar during late December 1994 and January 1995, the administration proposed $40 billion in loan guarantees to help stabilize the Mexican economy. The President's support for the package met most of the criteria outlined at the start of this chapter. He warned of the security consequences of the Mexican crisis and described the loan guarantees as "vital to our interests."[16] He pointed to the domestic economic benefits of the proposal, noting that over 700,000 American jobs relied on trade with Mexico. He reached out to both parties in Congress, inviting Speaker Gingrich and Senate Majority Leader Dole to the White House early in the process and obtaining a pledge of cooperation from both of them. He signalled the package as a clear priority and deployed key administration economic officials to Capitol Hill. Even with all these efforts, opposition deepened among members of both parties in Congress. On January 31, after receiving word from congressional leaders that Hill approval would take additional weeks and might not come at all, the President announced that he had restructured the package in a way that would not require congressional action.

To be sure, the Mexican loan guarantee package is not a typical national security issue and bears little resemblance to the East-West battles of the Cold War. Indeed, the public and Congress may view it as a domestic financial matter as much as a foreign challenge. Yet the administration's abandonment of its initial proposal may mark a watershed in relations between the two branches on foreign policy. Congress's strong resistance to the first loan guarantee proposal underscores the importance of

---

[16] Ann Devroy and Kevin Merida, "President Makes Push for Support of Financial Rescue Package for Mexico," *The Washington Post* (January 19, 1994), p. A6.

many factors identified in this study, such as economic worries and concern over the deficit. Especially evident was the strong role of the freshmen in blocking the proposal. When Pat Buchanan called a press conference to denounce the package as a sop to Wall Street and foreigners, seven Republicans joined him or voiced their support; four were freshmen. The president of the 73-member Republican freshman class reported "almost unanimous" opposition to the administration's revised package among the new GOP members.[17]

Even though Congress is becoming more assertive, Capitol Hill is not about to start dominating American foreign policy. It is impossible for 535 separate sovereigns to do so (even though a few of them sometimes try). Rather, Congress will resist executive branch initiatives somewhat more strongly and more frequently than in the past. Periodically, Congress also will press specific initiatives on the White House, as it has its proposal to lift the Bosnian arms embargo, or its successful insistence in May 1995 that the State Department issue a visitor visa to President Lee Teng-hui of Taiwan. Congress's greater assertiveness is likely to affect the executive branch's behavior in systematic ways. It may, for example, force the White House to choose between spending more political capital on persuading Congress of its case, as it did on the aid package for Russia and the NIS, or bypassing Congress, as it ultimately did on the Mexico package or on its military occupation of Haiti.

Recommendations

If these conclusions are right, then there is little use in arguing, as some pundits and politicians have, that Congress should yield power over national security back to the presidency. Such King Canute-like exhortations will do little to halt the rising tide of congressional assertiveness in international affairs. Nor is it likely that the executive branch can get its way with Congress on an expanded national security agenda simply by mounting a more rigorous sales effort. The preceding chapters demonstrate that

---

[17] Kevin Merida, "Hill Critics Assail Clinton Initiative to Bolster Mexico's" Economy, *The Washington Post* (February 2, 1995), p. A6.

shrinking budgets and expanding domestic worries limit the number of such hard-sell jobs in foreign affairs, and that the security and economic stakes in what is being sold inevitably affect the quality of the sales pitch. There are, nonetheless, steps that leaders in both Congress and the executive can and should take to improve the quality of the relationship between the two branches, ensure that U.S. national security policies rest on informed public support, and strengthen American leadership in global affairs.

Focus more on core security concerns. Over the next decade, the United States faces pivotal choices about the core of its security policies, including relations with Russia, security agreements across the Atlantic and within Europe, U.S. economic and security relations with Asia, efforts to combat the proliferation of weapons of mass destruction, the expansion of global trade, and the readiness of the U.S. armed forces. These questions, each vital to America's security, should be the focus of intense dialogue between the two branches. For example, despite the early support from both the administration and congressional Republicans for expanding NATO's membership, far more public discussion is necessary before Americans understand and accept the costs and security obligations that such an initiative entails.

There is a danger that other issues—less important to America's security and highly divisive—will dominate the agenda instead. These include peacekeeping, population programs, and the global environment. Such programs have become the wedge issues of foreign policy—matters that have less direct importance for U.S. security but that can be used politically to polarize debate. Excessive focus on such issues will displace attention and reduce support for the more central security questions of this era, just as the Clinton administration's early efforts to lift the ban on homosexuals in the military undermined its overall relations with the military during a difficult period of downsizing. It is in the nation's interest for leaders in both branches to seek early, bipartisan compromises and understandings on less important security questions so that they and the public can focus more attention on the core security choices.

This is not to say that the United States should stop paying peacekeeping assessments, accept exploding global population rates, and ignore the hole in the ozone layer. It shouldn't.

Moreover, current tensions and debates on the proper place of such programs—even if driven by partisanship—are not only inevitable but healthy. But as this study demonstrates, such issues are likely to spur substantial congressional resistance and require inordinate political effort by the executive branch. It is hardly in the national interest to pursue such issues in an absolutist, polarized manner that puts them at the center of congressional foreign policy debates.

Substantially revise the War Powers Resolution and reach new understandings on peacekeeping. One way to reduce the time spent by both branches on tangential, divisive matters is by repealing most portions of the War Powers Resolution. For years, congressional debates about military deployments were filled with discussion of whether the president was obligated to invoke the Resolution. The resulting focus on the *process* of military engagement may have served the interests of members who preferred to avoid the political risks of debating the actual merits of the mission. The public was less well served, however, by this focus. Ultimately, the Resolution did little or nothing to limit the executive branch's war-making power. Presidents uniformly refused to accept the constitutionality of the law's key provisions. The courts, for various reasons, refused to enforce the law's 60-to-90 day limit on unauthorized deployments.

Even though, as noted earlier, Congress now appears to spend less time trying to apply the Resolution to various military deployments, the law continues to distort dialogue between the two branches. For example, certain aspects of the statute, including the 60-90 day "clock," are triggered when an administration declares that U.S. troops have been "introduced into hostilities or into situations where imminent involvement in hostilities is clearly indicated by the circumstances." As a result, the law continues to encourage administrations of both parties to avoid declaring that U.S. troops have been introduced into hostilities even when that is obviously the case.

Given that the War Powers Resolution distorts the national security dialogue between the branches, encourages Congress to avoid debating the merits of military actions, and fails to affect the executive branch's use of the military, Congress should repeal the toughest sounding but least heeded portion of the Resolution:

the 60-90 day clock. As noted earlier, proposals to repeal this and most other parts of the Resolution (except for its requirements for the White House to consult and report on military interventions) were introduced in the 104th Congress but—despite a strong plea by Speaker Gingrich—rejected in the House in June 1995.

It should not be surprising that a newly assertive Congress would balk at surrendering the War Powers Resolution, however ineffective it has been, or that many in the Republican majority would hesitate to give a Democratic president a freer hand, or even to appear to do so. The question is whether there is a way to overcome these obstacles. One answer may lie in another set of proposals under consideration in Congress—those regarding peacekeeping. Many of the specific peacekeeping restrictions that have been proposed by Sen. Dole and House Republicans are problematic. For example, by requiring that the cost of all U.S. military activities in support of peacekeeping be offset against U.S. peacekeeping assessment bills, those proposals effectively could end U.S. payments for international peacekeeping. President Clinton's threat to veto such legislation is well-founded. The administration, however, should view the peacekeeping provisions in Sen. Dole's bill and similar ones passed by the House as more than veto bait. It should use these provisions as the point of departure for negotiations between the two branches about the uses and limits of peacekeeping. For example, if the administration can reach agreements on how to square peacekeeping accounts with peacekeeping commitments, it could reduce a constant source of irritation between the branches and leave more room for discussion of vital security questions.

With new measures to address its concerns over peacekeeping, Congress might be more willing to repeal the 60–90 day clock in the War Powers Resolution. To this end, a greatly revised War Powers Resolution could specify new processes, such as the creation of a consultative group of congressional leaders. Such a mechanism could improve the dialogue between the branches, not only on actual deployments of U.S. troops, but also on potential deployments, peacekeeping, and regional "hot spots" that are unlikely to involve U.S. military force. Such a consultative group was the centerpiece of a proposal by Senators Byrd, Mitchell, Nunn, and Warner.

There are some actions that the executive branch can take unilaterally to ease tensions on these issues. Over the past two years, the Clinton administration initiated a series of closed, classified meetings between the President's top five security advisers—the secretaries of State and Defense, the chairman of the Joint Chiefs of Staff, the U.S. ambassador to the United Nations, and the national security adviser—with Congress's bipartisan leadership and the chairs and ranking members of the relevant committees. While the meetings have been a significant addition to the consultative process, they have occurred only three times with the House and twice with the Senate. This administration and its successors should continue these meetings and make them more regular—perhaps holding them once every two or three months. The monthly staff briefings on the UN calendar, initiated in 1993 by Ambassador Albright, also should be continued.

Find ways to bring more freshmen and junior members into the dialogue. The 236 Senators and Representatives who have joined Congress since the Berlin Wall fell will have a substantial impact on the future of U.S. national security policy. They are likely to be around for years to come (notwithstanding talk about term limits and current rates of turnover) and they appear to have distinct views about the world. It is important that those members and their views be well integrated into the national security policy process.

Yet junior members are underrepresented on the committees and subcommittees that address national security. For example, although members elected since 1989 account for 51 percent of the House, they account for only 36 percent of the total members on that chamber's various national security panels. Looking at the same problem from another angle, only 28 percent (61 of the 220) House members elected after 1989 sit on subcommittees or committees that would involve them in the details of national security issues.

Clearly, members of Congress can obtain information about world events without sitting on these committees. Nor is there reason to believe Congress's newer members are naive or ill-informed about America's security needs. Yet the high level of turnover in Congress in recent years suggests a need for additional ways to bring newer members into the national security dialogue between the branches. Leaders in both branches can play a role. The executive branch should provide regular briefings for the newcomers on national security issues. The Clinton administration has attempted to initiate such a process; it should regularize the practice. Leaders in both branches should create orientation activities on the national security process for new members, including tours of the White House situation room, the Pentagon, CIA headquarters, and the State Department.

Congressional leaders also can find opportunities for the newer members to participate in events that focus on foreign affairs, such as meetings with world leaders, appointment to congressional advisory panels on security issues, and participation in congressional delegations abroad. The leaders should give strong consideration to rotating freshmen onto the intelligence committees as new positions open. Congress also should consider creating a few rotating positions for freshmen on the foreign affairs committees that would not count against these members' limits for committee assignments. While such a move would contradict the recent thrust of congressional reform efforts, which have sought to reduce the proliferation of committee assignments, this would be a deserving exception. It would constitute a recognition that national security policy is fundamentally different from domestic policy, and that it is hard for members to learn enough about foreign affairs solely from experiences in their districts.

Greater effort by internationalist leaders to build the case for international programs. Ultimately, the great choice facing leaders in both branches and both parties is how much political capital they will use to build the case for national security initiatives in the face of the many pressures against such programs. After World War II, national leaders could point to the Soviet threat to mobilize support for such efforts. No comparable threat exists today. Leaders who believe that America's global engagement and leadership nonetheless remain imperative need to spend more time and energy persuading their colleagues and the public of their case.

Already, prominent Democratic and Republican voices have raised a cautionary flag against a hasty withdrawal from America's international commitments. President Clinton has made the call for continued engagement a staple of his statements on foreign policy. Former President Bush, in a speech soon after the November election, railed against Ross Perot and other "quasi-

isolationists" for their "faulted siren's call."[18]   Other leading
national security writers and former administration officials from
both political parties have sounded similar notes.

On occasion, such figures have banded together to defend particular initiatives, such as when three former Presidents, Ford,
Carter and Bush, joined several former cabinet-level officials to
help launch President Clinton's drive for congressional approval of
NAFTA. Such officials now should consider launching a broader,
more sustained effort, aimed at mobilizing public support for the
full range of American activities abroad. The challenge will be
defining "full range"; such public leaders surely will have strong
and differing views about the size and purpose America's national
security agenda. The key to such an effort will consist of putting
aside the most divisive initiatives and focusing on certain generic
categories of programs—humanitarian aid or denuclearization—
around which a broad consensus exists. If it is not yet possible to
reassemble the many spokes of national security policy around a
central theme after the Cold War, a distinguished group of public
leaders may at least be able to strengthen the case that support
for today's jumble of national security initiatives is essential.

One temptation is to seek changes in the congressional budget
process that might favor international programs in the face of
deficit-cutting pressures. Some of the possibilities include: merg-
ing the appropriations subcommittees on foreign operations and
defense; moving peacekeeping and other UN accounts out of the
Commerce-Justice-State appropriations subcommittee into the
Foreign Operations subcommittee; or restoring the "firewalls"
that existed from 1990-93 between defense, international affairs,
and domestic programs, so that national security programs cannot be raided to fund domestic priorities.

But such reforms are unlikely to happen or work. The experience on peacekeeping shows how difficult it is to change the
jurisdiction of appropriations subcommittees. The Clinton
administration's proposal to shift the peacekeeping account from
the CJS to the Foreign Operations appropriations subcommittees
found no takers on Capitol Hill. If the executive branch and

[18] Peter James Spielmann, "Former President Bush Lashes Out at Rise of
'Isolationists' in U.S.," *Associated Press* (November 23, 1994).

Congress could not agree on such changes when both were Democratic, then they are even less likely to do so now, with divided partisan control of the two branches. The peacekeeping experience also casts doubt on the efficacy of such reforms: attempts to fund this international program out of a different, larger pot—the defense budget—did little to increase political and financial backing for the activity and may even have undermined support. Finally, both case studies suggest that budget reforms are not strictly necessary to obtain adequate funding for national security programs. When a compelling case was assembled, Congress quickly found ways to bend the budget process to find funds for both the 1993 Russia/NIS aid package and the peacekeeping supplemental in 1994.

If the American public wants to swap fewer guns (or blue helmets) for more butter, there is probably little in the way of budget reforms that can stop them. In a democracy, this is as it should be. What America's international programs need in order to survive and succeed is not new budget rules, but new political will. The case for U.S. efforts abroad must be made, almost from scratch, to a Congress and public that bore the burdens of the Cold War and have proved willing to bear new burdens—but only if those burdens have visible links to American needs, interests, and purposes. That Congress and the public have insisted on these clear links reflects neither selfishness nor stinginess. "Show me" pragmatism lies at the heart of American politics. The sound coming from the new Congress is not a blind call for retreat so much as a firm demand to be shown the goals and rewards of American leadership in a new world.

Appendix

Much of the analysis in Chapter 1 involves contested national security votes from 1974 through 1994—that is, roll call votes in the Senate and House on which the executive branch declared a position, as recorded by the *Congressional Quarterly*. This study relied on the following guidelines in deciding which votes involved "national security" issues:

- As noted in the text, national security was defined to include foreign policy, defense, intelligence, and trade.

- Votes on nominations of national security officials were not included.

- Votes on adoption of rules for House consideration of national security bills were not included.

- Votes regarding budget resolutions, supplemental appropriations, recisions, or other general spending measures were not included unless national security functions accounted for more than half of the total funds involved in the amendment or resolution (thus, final votes on budget resolutions were omitted, but a proposed amendment to a budget resolution to reduce defense spending was included). Votes on the overall Commerce-Justice-State appropriations bills, however, were included.

- Votes on the following substantive areas were not included:
  —treaties on taxation, fisheries, or technical commercial matters;
  —treaties on extradition or other criminal matters;
  —policies or benefits relating to veterans;
  —trade adjustment policy or funding;
  —defense conversion or aid to displaced defense workers;
  —energy conservation;
  —immigration.

Acknowledgments

This study was made possible by a great deal of debt and very little equity. The debt I owe to all who lent their ideas and assistance to this volume. There is hardly any equity, because all I give them is my thanks. But let me at least do that.

Above all, I appreciate the support of Morton Abramowitz and the Carnegie Endowment for International Peace. Ever since I arrived at Carnegie after leaving the National Security Council, it has felt like I drew to an inside straight—lucky, exciting, and rewarding. I thank Mort for dealing me in, and my colleagues for the stimulation of their company.

This study benefitted greatly from comments on early drafts by members of a Carnegie study group on Congress and national security. The group was chaired by the Stimson Center's Barry Blechman and convened with the assistance of Alton Frye of the Council on Foreign Relations, Thomas Mann of The Brookings Institution, and Norman Ornstein of the American Enterprise Institute. Other participants included: Marjorie Browne, Richard D'Amato, Charles Flickner, Toby Gati, Richard Haass, James Hoagland, John Isaacs, Edward King, Richard Kirschten, Thomas Lippman, Janet Mullins, Terry Peel, Thomas Simons, Larry Smith, and Pat Towell. I thank them all for their time and insights.

I also want to express my gratitude to several people who took the time to provide detailed comments on full drafts of the book: Elliott Feldman, whose careful eye has guided my work for some 17 years; Maxine Isaacs; James Lindsay; study group members John Isaacs, Thomas Mann, and Norman Ornstein; and Carnegie's Morton Abramowitz and Christoph Bertram.

The case studies in this book were based, in part, on interviews with over 30 administration officials, members of Congress, and key congressional staff. While I committed to withhold their names, I want to thank them for their candid and thoughtful observations.

Carnegie Junior Fellow Brian Weinberger deserves special mention and thanks. Brian built our data base on congressional voting, crunched endless runs of numbers, researched legislative histories, and chased after obscure facts—and did it all with diligence, intelligence, and good cheer. His tireless efforts were literally indispensable.

Several others made important contributions as the study moved from note pad to printing press. Carnegie's Valeriana Kallab guided the production process and provided valuable comments on content and style. Gareth Cook provide excellent copy editing. Jennifer Little, Kathleen Daly, and Christopher Henley of Carnegie's library staff patiently and skillfully responded to my endless research requests. Rebecca Young and Sandy Shuster helped with meetings, mailings, and other aspects of the project. To each, many thanks.

My greatest debt, however, is to my wife, Laurie Duker, and my children, Sarah and Jacob, who have inspired and sustained me throughout my work on this study, during my time at the National Security Council, and across many ventures before that. Laurie is also my best editor and resource for understanding Congress. She began working with the institution long before I did and first made sense of it for me when I came to Washington. Over a dozen years ago, before we ever met, when I was first examining Congress as a graduate student in Boston, I called Common Cause to get some data on congressional campaigns. My call was directed to a staffer, and as I was told the name, I wrote on a piece of paper: "Laurie Duker's the one." She sure is, and this book is dedicated to her.

THE CARNEGIE ENDOWMENT FOR INTERNATIONAL PEACE

The Carnegie Endowment for International Peace was established in 1910 in Washington, D.C., with a gift from Andrew Carnegie. As a tax-exempt operating (not grant-making) foundation, the Endowment conducts programs of research, discussion, publication, and education in international affairs and U.S. foreign policy. The Endowment publishes the quarterly magazine, *Foreign Policy*.

Carnegie's Senior and resident associates—whose backgrounds include government, journalism, law, academia, and public affairs—bring to their work substantial first-hand experience in foreign policy through writing, public and media appearances, study groups, and conferences. Carnegie associates seek to invigorate and extend both expert and public discussion on a wide range of international issues, including worldwide migration, nonproliferation, regional conflicts, multilateralism, democracy-building, and the use of force. The Endowment also engages in and encourages projects designed to foster innovative contributions in international affairs.

In 1993, the Carnegie Endowment opened the Center for Russian and Eurasian Studies in Moscow. Through joint projects on issues of common interest, Carnegie associates and researchers at the Moscow Center are working with Washington-based Carnegie associates to enrich intellectual and policy debate in the United States as well as in Russia and other post-Soviet states.

The Endowment normally does not take institutional positions on public policy issues. It supports its activities principally from its own resources, supplemented by nongovernmental, philanthropic grants.

Carnegie Endowment for International Peace
2400 N Street, N.W.
Washington, D.C. 20037
Tel.: (202)-862-7900
Fax: (202)-862-2610